GREEK PROVERBS

AND OTHER

POPULAR SAYINGS

CONTRIBUTORS

George Pilitsis
Andreas Papadatos
Maria Zafiris
Sam Chekwas

SEABURN

New York, Thessaloniki

ISBN: 1-885778-23-6

Library of Congress Cataloging-in-Publication Data

Cover design by Sam Chekwas
Typesetting & Layout, M&K, PO Box 1114, New York, NY 10037

Seaburn Books are sold to schools and institutions of higher learning at
discount prices. Seaburn Publishes books in English, Greek and Spanish
languages and also offers cassettes.
Seaburn Books books are sold through major distributors.
For more information call (718) 274-1300 or write to:
Seaburn Publishing,
PO Box 2085, LIC, New York 11102.

$\mathscr{C}$ONTENTS

$\mathscr{F}$OREWORD

Proverbs have been defined as a type of folk literature which in the form of brief and short sentences express a prodigious view of life and human experience. Greek proverbs, like the proverbs of almost every nation and ethnic group, embody the wisdom and wit of all people, from the simple folk of a village community, to the more sophisticated people of towns and cities. Moreover, they reveal people's way of thinking, and reflect conditions under which people function in their environment.

A careful study of proverbs will show that they are commentaries of social, economic and religious conditions of life. Moreover, they express people's hopes, fears, beliefs, prejudices and aspirations in life. There is hardly a life situation that proverbs do not comment upon in some way. They may be witty, sarcastic, humorous, admonitory, complimentary, preemptory, approving or rebuking. In this way, they may exercise a form of control regarding social behavior among the members of the community which produces them.

The present volume contains over a thousand memorable proverbs and other popular sayings from various parts of Greece. They consist mostly of short passages, often no more than two lines. Most of these proverbs are well-known or familiar to people and have been quoted many times over by editors and authors of similar books. They are the product of a culture that traces its origin in the distant past. While most of them reflect a culture of contemporary times, there are others that, in some details at least, are remarkably similar to those found in the writings of Classical antiquity as well as in the literature of Byzantine and post-Byzantine times, to a more recent past of Greek history.

The volume aims not only to enliven and enlighten the reader, but in the process also to entertain. It is our hope that the proverbs selected and presented here in the English translation will enjoy the appreciation of all readers, especially those who may not be familiar with the Greek language. Greece has made enormous contributions to our civilization. The Greek language has been a inexhaustible reservoirs of inspiration for world literature and science and will continue to influence our thoughts and creativity for years to come. I can only hope that more people will find the interest that I found in the language and study it.

Sam Chekwas, *Author*
Greece, A Life Time Dream

GENERAL

The world is not lost.
>It's not the end of the world.

He took the crooked path.
>He deviated from the right path in life.

He is a crooked wood of a man.
>He is an obstinate, pig-headed and stubborn individual.

And the blind man's right.
>Give the devil his due; lets be fair.

He is a strong glass.
>He is a heavy drinker; he can hold his liquor.

His sword cuts.
>His word carries weight; he can pull strings.

He is a sword of a man.
>He is on the level, a man who keeps his word; a trustworthy person.

Like in your own home.
>Make yourself comfortable; make yourself at home.

It was the drop that made the glass overflow.
>It was the last straw. The straw that broke the camel's back.

He catches birds in mid-air.
>He is a very smart and capable person.

He has even the bird's milk.
>He lives in great luxury. He lives off the fat of the land.

The bird has flown.
>You have missed your chance.

His hands catch.
>He is a very handy man.

He gives it by the eye-dropper.
> He is a tight-fisted person, a miser, a scrooge.

His pocket cannot bear it. (It's too heavy for his pocket).
> He cannot afford it.

He does not carry jokes.
> He is a no-nonsense man.

He has them in his pocket.
> He has control over them.
> He can make people do whatever he wants.

He/she is pecked.
> He/she is in love, or has a crush on somebody.

Whatever the rain brings down.
> Let things rip; come what may.

The walking stick has two ends; one belongs to the guest, the other belongs to the host.
> There are two sides to the story.
> Two people can play the same game.

He's eaten handfuls of gun-powder.
> He is a battle-hardened man.
> He is a very experienced man.

He became gun-powder.
> He blew his top; he got very angry.

He's got an uncle in the crown.
> This is said about people who have powerful patrons.

He found his craftsman.
> He met his match.

They got a whiff of him.
> He was caught in the act; they got wind of him.

They hung bells on him.
>He has done something so notorious that he became the
talk of the town.

He turned my head into a bell.
>He talked my head off; he gave me a headache.

When the cellar is full, the table is set easily.
>When we have the necessary provisions, it's easy to accomplish
an undertaking.
>When you have the money, you can start any business.

He is used to being naked, and is ashamed to be seen dressed.
>Some habits are hard to break.
>Some people have difficulty adjusting to changes.

He sits on my neck.
>He is a burden to me. He is bothering me.
>I have to put up with him.

The thief saw the lion and ran away.
>A liar is worse than a thief.

He is a great pestle.
>He is a numskull, a jerk, a nitwit.

Businesses are not built with lies.
>You cannot start any kind of project without money.

Rotten eggs do not hatch chicks.
>It is said about disabled parents who cannot produce children.
Also, we should not expect fine or brilliant ideas to come from
people who are not very smart.

He builds castles in the sand.
>He wastes his time with plans that will never materialize.
>His projects have no foundation.

He lights fires.
>He stirs up trouble. He fans the fire.

You should light him a candle.
You should be grateful for what he did for you.

His mouth goes like a carding machine.
He is a chatter-box; an important person.

He is a baked man.
He is an experienced, mature, ripe seasoned man.

I have him baked.
I talked him into doing something for me. He is my man.

Young children, small troubles; older children, bigger troubles.
Parent's concerns over children increases as the children grow older.

Don't pull out a tongue on me.
Don't give me lip. Don't talk back.

Bite your tongue.
May what you've just said never come true.

He pulls it off like a Spartan.
He is roughing it.

He exposed her on a twig.
He made her an experienced woman. He gave her a bad name. He ruined her reputation.

He squeezed out our oil.
He gave us a hard time.
He put a lot of pressure on us.

His screw has turned.
He's got a screw loose. He is off his rocker. He is insane.

What a missile of a man.
What a stupid, weird, screwy man!

He makes an ox out of a fly.
He makes a mountain out of a molehill.

Where are you grazing?
Where is your mind wandering? Why aren't you paying
attention?

He/she has gone downhill.
They became involved with the wrong people.
They have ruined their reputation.

They made ground meat out of him.
They made mince-meat of him. They beat him to a pulp.

Like seeks like and manure the vegetables.
People of the same kind tend to stay together.
Birds of a feather flock together.

Everybody, even crippled Maria.
Everybody with no exception. Tom, Dick and Harry.
When unqualified people get involved with things.

When you keep a lame man company, you learn to limp.
It is said to show the influence some people have on others.
It also shows how strong peer pressure can be.

He is a log of a man.
He is a blockhead, an ignorant and uneducated person.

Oh! Burst up!
Oh, shut up!

If you don't have fingernails to scratch yourself...
We must rely on our strength and qualifications ... and not
expect others to do things for us. We must learn to be self-
sufficient.

He sharpens his fingernails.
He is cruising for a bruising. He is getting ready for a fight.

He made her into a rag.
He tore her reputation to shreds. He humiliated her.
He wiped the floor with her.

He made porridge out of my brains.
>He talked my head off.

Koutrouli's wedding.
>An expression that shows great confusion. Mayhem.

He/she rides the reed.
>He/she went off his/her rocker.

He drowns in the shallows.
>He loses his head at the slightest adversity.
>He gives up easily at everything he undertakes.

They are tatsi-mitsi-kotsi.
>An expression used to show how close two people are.
>They are hand in glove; They are two peas in a pod.

He speaks without a bridle in his mouth.
>He doesn't mince his words. He speaks without restraint.

He doesn't give away chestnuts.
>He is demanding and inflexible.

A curse on two things: poverty and old age.
>Poverty and old age are two things people want to avoid at all costs.

When the old lady got pregnant, she drew the bolt.
>Some people take precautions only when it's too late.
>He locked the barn door after the horse was gone.

He made us pregnant.
>He talked our heads off. He pestered us with no mercy.

He was saved by a hair.
>He had a narrow escape.
>He was saved by the skin of his teeth.

He who laughs last, laughs best.
>About a person who succeeds after an apparent defeat.
>He has the last laugh.

Like the crazy woman's hair.
>   Things are topsy-turvy; everything is in a tangle.

He chanted him a handful.
>   He gave him a piece of his mind.

Her tongue moves like a spinning wheel.
>   A very talkative person who doesn't know when to stop talking.

Your brains and a sovereign.
>   It is said to a foolish and silly person who makes no sense in what he says.

Air got into his brain.
>   He has a swollen head. He is full of himself.

He dresses to the hair.
>   He is always well-dressed; he is shipshape.

Everything went to the thunder.
>   It was all in vain!

I play him on my fingers.
>   I twist him 'round my finger.

Where you live is your fatherland.
>   One owes his allegiance to the country where he lives.

He who pays for the violin chooses the song.
>   He who has the upper hand has priorities.

He changed his violin.
>   He changed his tune; He changed his mind about something.

Too many midwives pull out the baby deformed.
>   Too many cooks spoil the broth.

Too many captains sink the ship.
>   Too many cooks spoil the broth.

Iron welds when it's hot.
>Strike when its hot.
>Whatever you can do today don't leave for tomorrow.

Proverbs are the wisdom of the street.
>Proverbs are the people's voice born from life's experiences.

They will dance the dance of Isaiah.
>This is said when two people are about to get married.

He made a sea of things.
>He made a mess of things.

He is beating the sea.
>He is beating a dead horse. He is ploughing the sand.
>He wastes his time.

He needs a wet plank.
>He needs a spanking; He deserves a sound thrashing.

He made a wine-skin out of him in a beating.
>He gave him a severe beating. He tanned his hide.

It's raining by the bucketful; It rains chair-legs.
>It rains a great deal; it's coming down in sheets; its pouring.

There isn't a drop of saliva.
>To be without money; to be flat broke; down to the last penny.

He is the last hole in the reed-pipe.
>He is very insignificant person. His opinion doesn't count.
>He is a man of little importance.

He has his belt undone for a quarrel.
>He has a chip on his shoulder; he is out to pick a fight.

If wishes were granted, even beggars would be noblemen.
>If wishes were horses, beggars might ride.
>Not all of our wishes are fulfilled in life.

The more you stir up shit, the more it stinks.
> Don't open up old wounds. Let bygones be bygones.
> Let sleeping dogs lie.

Remember your own (youth) and forgive your children.
> Don't be critical of your children for the mistakes they make.
> We all learn from our childhood mistakes.

Now in your old age, old man, get an education.
> Old habits die hard. It's hard to teach an old dog new tricks.

They will sit him on the bench.
> They will take him to court; they will prosecute him.

The cat brought the mouse as a witness.
> It is said about criminals or people in power who intimidate
> witnesses into testifying on their behalf.

The cesspool said to the chickencoop, "go away because you stink."
> This is said about people who point out other people's faults
> while ignoring their own. The pot calling the kettle black.

A grain of prudence is worth more than a barrel of gun-powder.
> Act wisely and do not give in to the destructive power of anger.

Love, though blind, strikes on open-eyed women.
> It is said about the power of love that even the most careful and
> smartest of people cannot resist or avoid it.

> *The first European civilization was developed in the third and
> second millenia BC in the Aegean islands, in Crete and around
> the Aegean. The first inhabitants were known as Pelasgians.*

MAN, WOMAN, AND ELDERS

The old woman found the figs so sweet, she even ate the fig leaves.
> Pleasures are desired by all, and the elderly are no exception.

Daughter, only your apron should sway against your husband.
> A woman should act according to the type of husband she has.
> A woman's expenses should be in line with her husband's capabilities.

Wife of the blind man, who are you dolled up for?
> It is said about the wife of an inferior man who is cheating on him or who plans to cheat.

Even the siever's wife peddles her husband.
> A wife may tend to glamorize her husband and make him appear greater than what he is.

I want a man, and I want him now.
> It is said about an impatient person who is very demanding.

They look at my husband and they pay me honor.
> A woman who has a good or a successful husband is honored in her social circle.

The old lady craved for melon in the middle of winter.
> It is said for odd appetites and cravings that are by nature impossible to obtain.

Every old man thinks his fart is a fragrance.
> Everybody thinks their faults are virtues.
> Everybody believes their thoughts and deeds are better than they actually are.

Even if an old lady gets made up, she is noticed by the uphill.
> It is said for those who try to act young.

The wind and a woman cannot be locked.
> A woman should have the freedom to decide on her own.
> An outraged woman is an ocean in fury.

A woman with a mind is like a treasure in the house.

    A good-minded woman is a great asset for a family.

A woman who laughs and accepts your gifts you may kiss as you wish.

    The romantic response of a woman: if a woman wants a man, she shows it by her actions.

When an old man is happy, his youth he reminisces.

    It is a characteristic of the elderly. When they are happy, happy moments of their youth come to mind.

Whoever does not listen to his elders falls wounded.

    He who does not take the advice of his elders bitterly regrets it. Following the advice of those who have experience, we are able to get closer to happiness.

Good for the old man that is restless, and the youth that sleeps.

    The elderly should not sleep a great deal, but the young should get a good rest.

Beautiful is beautiful, five and ten times over, but above all a good minded woman is more beautiful.

    It is great for a family to have a good-minded woman. She guides the family to success and she corrects her husband's faults.

A woman and a horse want a capable rider.

    A woman wants good and strong guidance, and a worthy and capable husband.

Never judge a woman before you marry her.

    The true character of a woman surfaces after the wedding.

The wife of the king is cursed in secrecy.

    They do not dare slander the wife of a powerful and prestigious man in the open. A woman can outsmart all.

A woman is a pond, a man is a river.

    A woman stays home, but the man is out conducting business. A man is usually more active than a woman.

The woman has caught the devil in her bun.
> A woman has cunning senses. She is by her nature cunning. She shows one thing, yet is ambitious for something else.

A good housewife is a servant and a lady.
> A good housewife may have many chores around the house, but she has many pleasures, too.

The love of an old man is better than the strikes of a young one.
> An older man who behaves well is better than a younger, irritable man.

A lazy youth is a poor old man.
> If we labor in our youth, we will have financial security during old age.
> When we have the strength for intensive labor, we secure a good life for when we grow old and are unable to work.

Every one is focused on the fight, but the old lady has her mind on the honey.
> The elderly are more worried about themselves, their health, and their nutrition.

He who holds an eagle by the tail and a woman by her word holds nothing.
> Unlike a man, a woman usually doesn't keep her word, nor does she have the stability that a man does. A woman's promise is an empty promise.

The more the old lady rushes, the more the yarn snaps.
> The more we rush, the more mistakes we make.
> He who rushes, stumbles.

The advice of the elders, and the knowledge of the scholars.
> Listen to the advice of the elderly, and the wisdom of the learned. The elders have more experience, and the scholars more knowledge.

Whatever I see before me, I tell it to my husband.
> About honorable and honest women, who value their husbands and offer them every success and possession they may have.

To the mean woman, even her hair is at fault.
>It is said about difficult people who find fault with everything.
>They nag and are agitated by the slightest thing.

Our master has a mistress, and our lady another man.
>It is said when a couple is not faithful to each other.

A bit of some and everything, a good housekeeper and his wife can handle.
>It is said when a couple manages financially, and has a good life.

He has the heart of a brave youth and the opinion of an old man.
>The characteristics of a successful and capable man are the vibrancy of youth and the wisdom of the years.

The old lady burned her tongue on the batter, and now she even blows on the yogurt.
>It is said about those who got hurt in the past, and now display great caution.
>Prior past experiences make you more cautious.

Come, grandpa, to show you your vineyard.
>It is said about an inexperienced person who thinks he knows more than others.
>To teach one's grandmother to cook eggs.

> *Greece entered the Bronze Age in 3000 BC and that era was called the Aegean civilization.*

HUMAN QUALITIES

The blind man was searching for a needle in the haystack, and the deaf man answered: I heard it drop.
> It is said about impossible things that can't be done.
> It is said when we try to do something beyond our capabilities.

By the time the scholar thinks, the mad man has crossed the bridge.
> Sometimes, daring people are more successful than those who contemplate or hesitate because of their intellectual or ethical convictions.

He who is not loved has bad breath.
> It is said about a person who is not well liked and is avoided at all costs, and is usually wrongfully slandered.

Whoever works like a slave, sleeps like a master.
> The person who works hard sleeps well at night, because he knows that his labors will bear him fruit.

The quick has grace.
> The quicker you complete a planned task, the better the results. Many delays usually hinder good results.

Before the gypsy was content, the drum had broken.
> Before a person has a chance to enjoy something he worked for, misfortune strikes. Before profit is gained, a setback happens.

We are all nuts, some more, some less.
> We all possess a degree of madness.
> We all have our flaws.

You dig up the soil, dust gets in your eyes.
> If you involve yourself in insignificant matters, you come out wrong in the end.

He who has a selective friend has a treasure.
> A good friend is priceless, and may prove to be helpful in times of need.
> A man knows who his friend are in times of danger and hardship.

Intelligence is worth more than strength.
> An intelligent person can accomplish more than a strong person.
> Strength, without intelligence, is worthless. It usually leads to
> faulty ends. The pen is mightier than the sword.

From a mayor to a clerk.
> It is said when someone loses his high position and ends up in a
> lower one than what he originally had.

A virtuous man can be noticed by his head, not by his years.
> Intelligence and morality are not always measured by age.
> Many young people act better than older people.

Light your lantern before night finds you.
(The children of the wise cook before they are hungry).
> It is better to be prepared.

He who eavesdrops hears his own disgraces.
> An eavesdropper usually hears others gossiping about him.

**It is better if a priest, a doctor, and a policeman never enter
your house.**
> When one of these people appear, something goes wrong.

The donkey grazes where he is tied.
> Each person should arrange his life according to the
> circumstances that arise.

He said it, paper and ink well.
> It is said when someone tells it like it is.
> He said it in great detail.

Sweet talk the naive person, so he can tell you all his secrets.
> Take good care and talk nicely to a naive person, and he'll tell
> you everything.
> A good hearted person shares his secrets because he has trust in
> his fellow man. Sweet talk will get you anything.

An illiterate man, a shabby piece of wood.
> An illiterate man is useless, much like a shabby piece of wood.
> An illiterate man can never produce as much as a literate one.

Truth without lies, food without salt.

Truth that lacks the slightest bit of falsification is not tasty.
Lies enhance what we say.
No truth is absolute; lies are the salt of truth.

From a child and from a crazy man you learn the truth.

This saying tells us that only from a spontaneous person we can
learn the truth. Children and fools speak the truth.

Need works skills.

Need makes a person more cunning, more aware and capable.
A person that has a true need tries to find ways to manage.

On a balding head, everyone plays barber.
(In the donkey's village, everyone acts like the doctor.)

It is said about those who take advantage of an unprotected and
weak person.
We pretend to know it all before an ailing and miserable person.

Pull me, even if I cry.

It is said about a person who wishes to do or to attain something,
even though he pretends not to, so he can get it easier in the
end.

A sick man needs a doctor, and a dead man needs tears.

A sick man needs medical help to get better, not cries and tears
that foretell his end.
The sick need medical attention the way the dead need mourning.

One boss is more than enough, and friends, few and by the plenty.

Try to have few bosses and many friends, because friends can
prove to be useful.

He who overextends himself must pull back quickly.

It is usually said for the merchants who open large trading, and
usually fall.
Whoever makes himself to appear greater than what he is, and
can only act on his true capabilities, fails.
He who climbs high falls down heavily.

When the emperor farts, his subjects overdo it.
>When people in a position of leadership don't act accordingly,
>people tend to imitate them.
>Incapable leaders who cannot function and lead the people are
>overthrown.

If you wash a black man to whiten him, you only waste your soap.
>Some situations cannot be changed, no matter how much you try.

Whoever hurries, stumbles.
>The person who rushes and is not careful can make mistakes.
>Rushing and improvising on a task, or in a situation, only leads
>to mistakes. Haste makes waste.

I laugh at twelve, and thirteen laugh at me.
>The lack of self knowledge and self respect.
>When we can't really understand the situation.

From the lips the word emerges, and it lands on thousands.
(The words lips and thousands are homonyms in the Greek language)
>It is said about gossip. Idle and malicious talk can hurt many.

You found your craftsman.
>When someone finds a person who outsmarts him and puts him
>in his place. Do not try to deceive a wise person.

Ask for an old doctor and a captain.
>It tells us that sometimes, experience is a great asset.
>Experience is the best teacher.

I came here a king, and I leave a gypsy.
>The misfortunes of our foolish attempts.
>(I went for wool, and I came out with a haircut)

The quarrel was for the quilt.
>When the fuss was over material things and economic gain.
>All the fuss was about who will come out shorn.
>To lose the shirt off your back.

Even the blind man's right should be spoken.
> The rights of the poor and the handicapped should be voiced.
> Even the poor and the handicapped have the same rights as everybody else.

He who thirsts sees water wells.
> The person that has needs seeks opportunities.
> We think and ache for the things we really need.

The dirty love the dirty.
> People of lower standards mingle with their equals.

Tell me who you keep company with, and I'll tell you who you are.
> We all try to interact with people equal to us.

The root-curer.
> The practical doctor.

Lies do not live to grow old.
> Lies are quickly uncovered.
> Nobody can depend on a lie; sooner or later he will have to face the truth and act accordingly.

Do not throw a stone in the well that quenched your thirst.
> Don't be ungrateful towards those that helped you.
> Don't bite the hand that feeds you.

He died on a straw mat.
> He died poor.
> He died forgotten and with many grievances.

An Armenian stay.
> A prolonged visit in a friendly environment.
> In the olden days, Armenians would stay for hours at a time on visits to friends' homes.

A necessary evil is bearable.
> Sometimes we withstand some misfortunes because we simply can't do anything about them.

He who looks way up high gets blinded.
> The person who is not well balanced in his search can do stupid things.

He made calculations without the inn keeper.
> When some one did not analyze something well.
> When we conclude one thing and something different happens.
> He makes plans without considering important details.

A good skipper proves himself in a storm.
> A good and capable person proves himself in times of trouble and hardship.

Better for your threshing floor to be small, and by itself.
> It is better to have your own business, no matter how small.
> It is usually said about merchants and businessmen.

He was boasting about a small boat, and he mounted a large vessel.
> You have to be sure about your actions and undertakings.

At the deaf man's door, knock all you want.
> You can talk and talk, but if the person you're talking to doesn't understand, or has no desire to understand, he will not respond.

The fare wakes up the muleteer.
> The expectation of profit always stirs our interests.
> This is usually said about merchants.

The lawyer doesn't need representation.
> The person who knows how to do his job well doesn't need advice from others.
> A well informed person can rely on his own knowledge.

If you have wealth, you also have a big tongue.
> Those who have great wealth are able to say what they please; furthermore, what they say sounds wise.

He who waits for others dines late.
> Everybody should rely on his own personal capabilities.

If I die of a cold, may it be ridden with curse and plague.
> Sometimes things of minor significance, as well as misfortune, bring us pain and sorrow.

Even the crippled man arrives in town slowly, and limping.
> With persistence and patience we can achieve anything.
> Even with minor capabilities, if we have patience, happiness is sure to follow.

Pity the one who is hungry and places hopes on his neighbors.
> Heartless neighbors do not help, even in your hour of need.
> Pity the person who relies on others.

Smart people do from the beginning what fools do at the end.
> Smart people assess a situation thoroughly from the beginning and then proceed accordingly.

He ate the iron rods.
> It is said about an angry person.
> It can be said about a person who tries anything and everything to succeed.

Neither voice, nor vision.
> When something, or someone doesn't say anything.
> Neither sound or sight.

The king is cursed behind his back.
> Bad-natured people curse their fellow man behind his back because they don't dare curse him to his face.

For the idle, everyday is a holiday.
> For the person who doesn't work or doesn't apply himself, everyday feels like a holiday.

He lost the compass.
> This is said when a person is very agitated, or when a person has no clue about what is going on.

My soul went to Koulouri.
> I was very frightened.

He's for the festivals.
>He is insignificant and silly.
>His purpose is foolish and weird.

Spanking came from paradise.
>Sometimes spanking has its benefits.
>Spare the rod and spoil the child.

Fear protects the meek.
>Aware of existing danger, we take a great deal more into consideration before acting in hopes of avoiding that danger.

A doll on the outside, a plague on the inside.
>One seems nice but has many faults. Looks may deceive.
>Good appearance, but a horrible personality.
>You cannot judge a book by its cover.

The one who laughs last, laughs best.
>The success of any undertaking can only be seen at the end.

Poverty eats money.
>When we find cheap things, we buy and buy, wasting our money.

Whoever nourishes himself with hopes dies of starvation.
>Sometimes our hopes and dreams let us down. We have to work and try hard to attain happiness.

My final bit of knowledge, if only I had you first.
>Experiences should become our lessons.
>We should learn from our experiences.

He is the captain of sweet water.
>A person boasting about himself is probably less capable of what he claims.

An entire year doesn't bring what one hour carries.
>Frequently, chances and disasters arise in a short span of time, whereas a long span of time can pass without any change or major development.

I shall dance him in the pan.
> I will torment him.

Education victors over nature.
> A person develops with knowledge and education.
> Education makes a person better and wiser.
> The educated person has more to gain than an illiterate man.

Step by step, you'll reach the peak.
> You will develop and succeed if you take it slow and act
> accordingly. Determination can lead to success.

There's one way of thinking in the village, and another way in the city.
> In small towns, because of the tight social circle, we care greatly
> about the opinion of others, and we don't act the way we should.

When you have, save, and when you lack, labor.
> Saving and laboring ensure a comfortable life.

It came to him like a pan.
> To be struck all of a heap.
> Like a bolt of lightning.
> It is said about a person who has an unavoidable accident.

Everybody else is with their madness, and he's with his umbrella.
> Every person is preoccupied with their own issues.
> We all have our hang-ups.

Out of the dance, they sing many songs.
> Everyone seems to have opinions on issues that don't involve
> them.

The wild came to chase away the tame.
> When a person tries to impose his narrow view and beliefs on a
> person of higher morality or wisdom.

When you're going, I'm coming.
> I have more experience in this matter.

A pointless mind makes double the effort.
>   Faulty efforts and decisions are sure to guide us to unnecessary
>   hardships and troubles.

The liar and the thief are happy the first year.
>   People with bad agendas are quickly uncovered.

A task without reward is punishment.
>   A task or work should always be rewarded.

With the soul in the mouth.
>   With great fear.

Need makes a person brave.
>   When a need exists, a person becomes fearless and brave to
>   confront the situation.

The cruel master whips me and I whip you.
>   It is said about people who tolerate the abuses of their superiors,
>   they turn around and abuse those under them.
>   This is a sign of a bad personality.

Even with its thousands of troubles, life is still sweet.
>   Despite all of the downfalls and hardships, life is still beautiful.

Whoever sows laziness, harvests hunger.
>   The lazy man is usually poor.
>   If we are lazy, we can never have economic gains.

He's an idiot with a helmet.
>   He is a big idiot.
>   His efforts and decisions are foolish.

My new sieve, where shall I hang you?
>   It is said about a person who has something new and takes
>   exceptional care of it.

Help him, so he can bring you down again.
>   It is said about an ungrateful person who doesn't appreciate the
>   help he receives from others.

Never help an insatiable or an ungrateful person.

We have to watch whom we help.

We only put ourselves out when we help a bad and an impudent person.

Listen to everything, and believe what you wish.

Usually, all that we hear is not related to the reality of the situation.

We must distinguish the truth from among the lies.

Better a coward than a dearly departed.

Sometimes, being a coward is the smart thing to do.

A coward avoids hardships and dangerous situations.

If you sit in your place, nobody can make you get up.

The people who don't involve themselves in the affairs of others, or don't undertake tasks that require more than they can give are not bothered by anyone.

Even a small gift has grace.

Even a gift that may not be of great value invokes gratitude.

Frequently, with a small gift we can accomplish big things.

If a clever person is fooled, he's fooled for a long time.

When a clever person is fooled by something or someone, he is fooled for good.

He who listens becomes wise, and he who speaks, regrets it.

The person that doesn't talk too much comes out a winner.

The gypsy saw his own kind, and his heart was exulted.

We are happy when we are among our kind.

When a person is in familiar surroundings, he feels at ease.

Better to be alone than with bad company.

It is better to be alone and have no worries, than to be with bad friends that may harm you.

Bad company usually leads us to misfortune.

A careful person can find happiness alone.

Illness comes on horseback, but leaves on foot.
> Illnesses come quickly, but leave slowly.

Whoever works like a king must have his mind on everything.
> High positions also have great responsibilities.
> The person that holds a high position must meet the demands of his position.

I told my friend the truth, and he became my enemy.
> When we voice the truth we become an annoyance.
> Most of the time, the truth is bitter.

If one bad thing happens, many more follow.
> Usually, one bad thing brings on other bad things.

His swan-song.
> His final deed or appearance.

The person that lives poor to die rich is crazy.
> This is about the people who have the means to live a good life, but deny themselves every pleasure; they are happy knowing that they have money even though they live like paupers.

Labor like a slave, and eat like a master.
> Work hard and diligently, and enjoy the fruits of your efforts.

A thousand good people can fit in a closet.
> People of good nature, even if they are many, always manage according to circumstance.

Divide and rule.
> When your opposition is divided, you can easily prevail.
> Divide and conquer.

He who wants more loses the little that he holds.
> Our greediness leads us to downfall.
> It is better to have one stable job.

Every smart-ass to his place.
> Every clever person should know his place.

He who questions never loses.
> A person is better off when he questions and seeks advice.

The person that honors the person next to him honors himself.
> Worthy and honorable behavior honors the person.
> When we show respect for others we show respect for ourselves.

He laid it all out for him, completely loose.
> He said it like it is.

Your blessing cracks stone.
> Your blessing is strong and helps me.

The gallant youth knows another path as well.
> A resourceful person knows how to handle a situation in many ways.
> There are a thousand ways to skin a cat.
> There are many ways that can help us out of difficult situations.

When the enemy leaves, everybody becomes a hero.
> When danger becomes distant, everybody acts strong.

He may lay carpets before you, but behind you he digs a grave.
> About people who act as friends, yet think evil about us.

I know you like a counterfeit dime.
> I know you well.
> I know you and how you operate.

I live here, yet I bake somewhere else.
> I live here, yet my job is somewhere else, helping others.

Madness doesn't seek the mountains.
> Irrational behavior is characteristic of humans.

Money is round and rolls.
> Money exchanges hands.
> Many rich people end up poor.

He who concentrates on his work gives a good life to his family.
>The person who works intensively and doesn't concern himself in the affairs of others always has money and provides a good life for his family.

How are your kids doing, black man? They're getting darker.
>It is said when our business is doing poorly or when everything seems to be getting worse.

They made it into a crisis of the Middle East.
>When an insignificant matter is escalated in significance, and it becomes annoying.

The person who fears to do many things does very little.
>The person who fears expanding his business or his social life has no gain.

If jealousy was mange, the entire country would be infested.
>This saying tries to note how innate jealousy is.

Teacher, although you taught the law, you didn't keep it.
>It is said about the person who says one thing and does another. For people who don't practice what they preach.

Love your friend with all his faults.
>We all have our faults. Therefore, it is only natural that our friends have theirs as well.
>We have to respect people, despite their faults.

Where there's a poor man, there his fate lies.
>It seems that all the misfortunes find the poor.
>Misery and misfortune keep a poor man company.

My oven, I built you, and I shall tear you down.
>It is said about the people who have a right to what they created and can act as they see fit.

Good accounts make good friends.
>Good communication helps mutual respect among people.
>Short reckoning makes long friends.

Five months he's grieving, and seven he's in sorrow.
> It is said about the people who are always suffering. These people are bad luck and are never able to attain happiness.

A person sees himself with different eyes than he sees the person next to him.
> We don't see our faults the way we see the faults of others.
> It is said when we enhance what we are capable of.

Many compliments are tiresome.
> Sometimes, many compliments are annoying and counterproductive.

Do not choose a doctor because he's your friend, but because he's the best.
> A good doctor is always useful. Good friends do not always make it unto the list of experts.

Whoever wastes time can never gather it again.
> The days and years slip away. We must seize every chance and opportunity we get.

As you have made your bed, so you must lie on it.
> Your results will be based on your actions and effort.
> We are responsible for our actions.

A thousand friends are nothing, when one is an enemy.
> One enemy is stronger than many friends, and he can harm us in the worst possible way.

May God save you from a bad neighbor.
> A neighbor that doesn't like us, and talks bad about us, can create bad situations.

Your laughter will result in bitterness.
> Now you are happy and you're laughing, but tomorrow you can be in tears.
> It is said when we don't consider what the end may hold.

An old enemy can never be a friend.
> It is foolish to befriend a person who in the past has harmed you.
> It is better to avoid a malign person.

In a thief's house, other thieves don't enter.

    Con-artists avoid the houses of others like themselves.

    The mutual respect among people of the same kind.

Let them call me Lady, even if I'm dying of hunger.

    As long as they think I'm important, it doesn't matter if I have no money.

    We all feel it is important to make a good impression.

The person who stares high up is quickly grounded.

    The person who boasts of himself is quickly humbled.

    The person who pretends to be what he is not has a sad end.

Luck is better than bravery.

    Luck is preferable over bravery. It is better to be a lucky coward.

Go get a haircut.

    What you're saying has no basis, it's stupid.

    We are not concerned with your efforts. Go jump in a lake.

On the ninth day of his death, another man entered his house.

    It is said in jest about impatient widows that cannot hold out.

The more you talk about yourself, the closer you reach to lies.

    Talking constantly about ourselves, we add lies so as to impress.

Show what you really are in one degree lower.

    A person should never assume a higher worth of what he is.

    Modesty is always a useful quality.

A good word costs nothing yet brings many benefits.

    With a positive attitude, we gain much more.

    Courtesy can bring you closer to happiness.

If I want to curse you, I can find a million reasons.

    We can find many reasons to bad-mouth a person.

    We don't need a real reason to scold someone.

If you don't have a friend, you only have one hand.

    A faithful friend is a sort of treasure.

    We can't succeed without friends.

Complete to the mind is knowledge.
>The smart person understands.
>Our education is enhanced by our cleverness.

Whatever you do on your own is quickly completed.
>Don't expect any results if you don't tend to something yourself.
>If you don't care about your work, don't expect any good results.

The gypsies love a scolding like they love a dance.
>Fools thrive on arguments.
>The gypsies have quarrels as festivals.

Freedom at a cost is much better than work with a reward.
>Liberty is most valued.

The world is a staircase; some ascend it, some descend it.
>In our society, some are successful and some are miserable.
>We are not all on the same emotional or economic level.

Converse with a respectful person and waste your wealth.
>When you interact with respectful people your time goes by with pleasure.

The rich man has the golden flutes, and the poor has the feast.
>Wealth doesn't always bring happiness.
>A person's good character and liveliness are valued more than money.

What blind man doesn't want his sight?
>We all hope for success and happiness.
>We all deserve the best in life.

A loaded wallet has many friends.
>Those who have money are usually surrounded by charmers.
>The person who has great wealth and spends it freely has many people around him.

We're sitting together, yet we are talking apart.
>It is said when people don't know how to communicate.

Hope for the best, expect the worst.
>   Be cautious with your optimism.

Test your friends when poverty strikes you.
>   When we are successful and rich, many pretend to be our friends.

The word is silver, silence is golden.
>   It is good to talk, but the one who doesn't say too much comes out to be the winner.

Never hang from only one hope.
>   We have to create many chances for wealth and happiness. Don't put all your eggs in one basket.

The one who goes to hunt in the marsh will be fooled.
(The person who falls into the chicken feed is pecked by the hens)
>   The person who gets involved with shady characters will surely get hurt.
>   The person who engages himself with useless causes never comes out winning.

If the clay is not molded, we will not have a brick.
>   It is impossible to have educated and capable people without effort and teaching.
>   Without effort and responsibility, we do not succeed at our work.

A person's desires are like the days; one comes when the other leaves.
>   Our desires are many; one follows the other.

Suffering becomes a lesson.
>   Experience is the best teacher. We learn from experience.

To the world it is like a drum, and to him it is a secret pride.
>   The whole world knows about it, yet he pretends to know nothing.

Nobility smells from afar.
>   The capable and noble man is noticed the first time we see him.

He who doesn't watch where he's stepping will fall in the mud.
> If we don't watch with whom we come into contact, we may find ourselves in trouble.
> If we are not careful with our efforts, we will suffer in the end.
> If we proceed at random, we will find trouble.

All doors open to courtesy.
> A courteous person is likable and easily accepted by others.
> A polite person is more likely to succeed.

Many hated wealth, none hated glory.
> Many people don't care about wealth, but they all seek glory.
> Glory is desired by most.

Unity makes strength.
> United we stand, divided we fall.

The good name is never forgotten.
> People with a good reputation are respected by others.

Better to have five in hand, than to wait for ten.
> It is better to have fewer, yet sure things, than many things in doubt.
> Better five birds in the hand than ten in the bush.

He builds castles in the air.
> He is laboring in vain.
> He is not sure about anything.
> He is not basing himself on reality.

One tastes bitter to him, and the other smells.
> When a person is not satisfied with anything.
> It is said about a hard-to-please person; a picky and fussy individual.

The kingdom stays in the family.
> Honors or faults are usually thought of being inherited.

He blows on it, yet it doesn't cool down.
> It already happened to him.
> When a person has realized the mistake a little too late.

Better poor and in health than rich and ill.
> Health has priority over wealth. Without health, we are not
> able to enjoy our wealth.

Everyone is a doctor, a musician and crazy.
> We find these three qualities, to some degree, in everybody.

He holds the few and loses the hundred weight.
> It is said about those who pretend to make a mistake, although
> they stand to gain from a certain situation.

Love and hate don't last for a long time.
> A philosophical view of these great human emotions.

Great kindness is also a humbling stupidity.
> The person who is too kind and doesn't look out for his own
> interests is stupid.

The one who is too choosy ends up with the scraps.
> The one who is way too picky has to settle for what ever is left
> over in the end.

A friend is seen in the hour of need.
> Good friends will be there to help when we need them.
> The person who has reliable and capable friends can be sure of
> success.

The truth always holds a lie, even if it is salted.
> Smart people should be able to distinguish the truth from the
> lie; then they can proceed with more certainty.

Too many words are poverty.
> Too much talk is often tiresome and often nonsense.

A man who takes up many skills lives in a bare house.
> People who attempt to learn many skills end up with no real
> knowledge at all. Jack of all trade, master of none.

Learn a skill and let it be, and if you're hungry, grab it.
> Whatever skill we learn may prove to be beneficial some day.

If you lost your way, ask or head back.
> If you fail at something you attempt, either seek the advice of someone who has experience, or simply walk away before you create more damage. Inform yourself so you won't make the same mistake again.

A beggar is the daughter of dissoluteness and waste.
> A beggar never has any success.
> A beggar is usually lazy and unmotivated.

Of all the evils, poverty weighs less.
> In other words, there are much worse things a person can be than poor.

Labor doesn't call for trouble, it calls for method.
> The people who understand their job and apply themselves nicely have less trouble and gain more rewards in the end.

Acquaintances of the madman, come and eat his wealth.
> It is said about the wasteful person of whom friends and relatives take advantage.

When crossing a bridge, dismount from the horse.
> When you are about to undertake a dangerous task, take careful and extra precautions.
> We have to be very careful in our actions when we encounter difficulties.

The child of a deaf woman never cries.
> Tough employers and foremen do not listen to the problems and complaints of the workers.
> Don't seek understanding from unsympathetic people.

A fine captain is of no use if he has a bad crew.
> The good businessman or corporate leader must have a good group behind him.
> In order to achieve, good leaders must have good followers.

A poor captain never has a rich voyage.
> A poor businessman doesn't receive great profits.
> A job that is poorly done doesn't produce anything positive.

He who digs a grave for someone else falls in it himself.
> Some of the time, fate works ironically. The people who plot and scheme the downfall of others tear themselves down instead. A bad action often backfires.

The thief screams to chase away the homeowner.
> It is said about a person who shows conceit and audacity. We say this when a person is at fault and tries to place the blame on others.

The hauler remembers God only when he's carrying a heavy load on his shoulders.
> We only remember and implore God when we find ourselves in a difficult situation.

One person lights the fire and another person fans it.
> One person usually starts the trouble, and somebody else then forces it and spreads it, sometimes harming even himself.

When you are high up, also look down.
> If you have honors and a high position, don't neglect the problems of others who are less fortunate than you.

The one who is persistent comes out a winner.
> Care and determination are needed if we are to achieve our goals.

Everything comes with time to a person who knows how to be patient.
> Happiness and fulfillment come to those who wait.

He squeezes stones and splits hair.
> It is said about a clever and wise person who knows what buttons to push to get what he wants.

Work has no shame.
> A person who makes contributions to society and receives fine rewards should be honored.

He buys and sells us.
> He is using us as he wishes.
> He is more clever and wiser than we are.

In your mind, you host a feast.
> You don't think rationally, and with your faulty conceptions and actions, you give others the wrong idea.

I come from Constantinople, and on the peaks there's cinnamon.
> Things that are incoherent; things that cannot be rationalized or ever actualized.

Speak kindly and it shall come.
> We should always be optimistic.

Speak few words with others, speak many with yourself.
> The person who thinks more than he speaks never loses.

You tied it into a knot.
> You're waiting for me to live up to my promise.
> You hold a grudge.

You by-passed us by fourteen generations.
> You're scolding us about things we are not responsible for.

Bronze head of Alexander the Great, the true King of Macedonia.

WEDDING - GROOM - BRIDE - LOVE

We left the wedding for evergreen oaks.
  It is said about a person who leaves a significant task for a
  pointless and worthless one.

Whatever the bride takes on horseback.
  Things happen and succeed if we ask and insist at the right
  moment.

Marriage is a lottery.
  Sometimes in a marriage we don't always get what we have
  hoped for.

The man who marries in his old age quickly flaps his ears.
  An old man may not be able to meet the demands and
  responsibilities of a marriage.

New brides came and molded new cookies.
  New people usually bring new ideas and methods to a house or a
  business.
  (Political parties change, and so do their decisions)

Love without spats and fits is not at all tasty.
  For a love affair to have interest, differences must exist
  between the two people. A love relationship without excitement
  is a boring affair.

Our bride kneads all the cracked loaves.
  When we place blame on others for no real reason.
  The bias we have about a certain person's abilities.

Better a wound-up widow than a miserable married woman.
  It is better for a woman to be a divorcee than to stay in a
  marriage that's full of pain and suffering.

The bachelor always sleeps with ease.
  Perhaps because he doesn't have the responsibility and the
  pressures of a family.

She fitted him with horns.
> This is said in reference to a wife who cheats on her husband.
> A man whose wife has committed adultery.

Either marry young or become a young monk.
> A person should marry young so he can meet the demands of a marriage. It takes a long time to get used to married life.

I tell it to the mother-in-law so that the daughter-in-law may hear it.
> When we say something to one person in the group so another can hear it. This is said when we want to give a subtle hint.

Who brags about the bride? Her snotty mother.
> Sometimes, the compliments of relatives stem from prejudice. This is said to show the partiality and bias of certain compliments.

He touched the magic wand.
> He fell in love.

The bald man's wedding.
> It is said when there's a big fuss or commotion going on.

I want her, even if she's a widow, poor and miserable.
> When we love somebody with all their faults .
> Love makes us see only the positive things in a person.

He/she stayed on the shelf.
> When a man or woman never marries.
> It is said about a spinster or an old bachelor.

Love is blind.
> Love only sees the good, not the bad.

When a couple separates, even the mountains crack.
> Divorce is one of the worst things for a family.

Those who marry in secrecy, are publicly disgraced.
> Something is wrong when a wedding takes place in secrecy.
> Marriage must be witnessed by relatives and other members of the community.

A married person regrets it once, a bachelor regrets it twice.
It is better to be married than to remain single.

With love, time passes, and love passes with time.
Love is wonderful, but may live only a short time.

We selected the bride who matches our generation.
It is said about a couple who is perfectly matched.
We always select the thing that suits us, and is most useful to us.

The groom is shaved towards the end.
The bill comes at the end. All the difficulties are at the end.
Everything has its price.

Beautiful women are desired, but the capable ones are praised.
Usually, men desire the company of beautiful women; however,
men say the kindest words about the capable ones.

The eye sees, and the heart catches fire.
Love first begins with the physical, then involves the emotions.

The people who are loved are frequently encountered.
When there's love and likeness between people, it is only
natural that they want to hang out together.

May the groom be from a good family with a good reputation.
The groom should be good and capable.

If the bride and groom want to, may the father-in-law be blind.
When two young people are in love, the in-laws cannot ruin the
wedding.
This is said also about people who are not dissuaded easily.

Without a groom, a wedding can't take place.
We can't achieve something if we are lacking the basic necessities.

He won't give his daughter, nor does he upset the would-be in-law.
This is said about a person who manages to get his job done
without upsetting anyone.

Everything went wrong at the wedding, and the bride was pregnant.
> When an obstacle comes out of nowhere.
> Things don't always happen as planned.

Find the bride and I'll stand up for you.
> The major achievements have priority. We must have the basic elements before we seek help from others.

A supported husband is a skinned fox.
> Keep away from mother-in-laws.
> It is better for each person to have his own house.

Invite him to your wedding so he can wish you "and again next year."
> It is said about a person who says things without thinking, and usually says the wrong thing at the wrong time.

The person who was not invited is seated last at the wedding.
> If a person who is not invited shows up, he is usually not welcomed.

The week is for the groom, and Sunday for the bride.
> Usually, a man takes his wife out on Sunday.
> Business before pleasure.

When a woman gets married, and when a horse is saddled, their wounds are seen.
> Faults appear after the wedding.

Married he's a clown, and single he's a spectacle.
> The situation is going from bad to worse.
> This is said about a person who cannot behave accordingly.

Paper and pen make the man a good groom.
> An educated man is the best candidate for a husband.

Love, a cough, and wealth can not be hidden.
> Certain things can not be concealed in life.

Whoever wins in cards loses in love.
> Lucky in cards, unlucky in love.

The bride, in all her finery, was stood up.
> Sometimes we prepare ourselves for something important and then receive unexpected bad results.
> All dressed up and nowhere to go.

They covered him with a hood.
> They forced him into marriage.

Neither a mother-in-law is a mother, nor a daughter-in-law a daughter.
> Genuine things can find no substitute.

They put the bread roll on him.
> He took the plunge; he got married.

Thirst married hunger.
> When two poor people get married.

Without bread, without wine, love freezes.
> With poverty, love slowly fades.
> Love has to have some basic elements to survive.

Someone paid for the bride.
> One person was to blame, and another person paid the price.

Love is a light that blinds my eyes and hides your faults.
> I cannot find fault with the person I love because I am greatly influenced by my emotions. Love is blind.

The bride doesn't collect the expense of the wedding.
> When the money we make from a certain business deal or job doesn't cover the expense we laid out, nor our efforts.
> It is said satirically when the bride is ugly.

Love is like a fresh egg, marriage is like a hard boiled egg, and divorce is like a shattered egg.
> The forms love can take.
> People's perceptions of various stages in marriage.

The best man's dog is welcomed, too.
> When we love a person, we should accept their friends as well.

INSECTS

He drains fat from the fly.
>It is said about a stingy person who is always looking to profit from every situation.
>To draw blood from a stone.

Even the ant carries its weight.
>Even the most insignificant person has his share of worries.
>No excuse for avoiding responsibility and commitment.

When God wants to destroy an ant, he places wings on it to fly.
>When a weak person is not able to take advantage of the opportunities that he finds, because they surpass his abilities.

He received whatever the fly carried on its wings.
>He ended up with the smallest profit possible.
>He got the short end of the stick.

Not all bees produce honey.
>Good people don't always do good deeds.
>Not all hard working people make a great amount of money.

Like a fly in the milk.
>He sticks out from his surroundings.
>He makes an impression.
>He sticks out like a sore thumb.

He even puts shoes on fleas.
>It is said about the clever and deceitful person.

For a flea's jump.
>With the slightest provocation.
>For the slightest reason.

A fly doesn't enter a closed mouth.
>This is said about careful and cautious people who don't believe everything they hear.
>A person who is not gullible.

From the skin of an ant, and from the fat of a mosquito.
>It is said about cheap and thrifty people who are always on the
>lookout for profit.

The flea was satisfied and came out onto the collar.
>Acquired new wealth.
>When we spend money to show off.

He acted like a dead bed-bug.
>He acted like nothing was going on.

He made the ant into an elephant.
>He exaggerated the situation.
>It is an insignificant issue that has taken on monstrous
>proportions. He made a mountain out of a molehill.

If you have nails, you will scratch, and if you don't, fleas will bite you.
>We should have the capabilities to fend for ourselves when
>we are faced with a difficulty.

Fleas got in his ears.
>Suspicions, for example, between a couple. He smells a rat.

The fly has made her threshing floor, and now she goes around scolding.
>It is said about people who are totally useless and yet, somehow,
>they succeed.

The fly ate iron and the mosquito, steel.
>It is said in jest about people who say they are going to do the
>impossible.

The flea eats from her master.
>The poor live from the service they provide to the wealthy.
>The worker who feels he gains from providing good service to
>his rich boss.

Even the mosquito gets in your nose.
>It is possible for the weak to get their revenge on those who
>suppress them.

For each word I told you, you swallowed a fly.
> You thought I was telling you the truth, when I was simply lying.
> It is said about gullible people.

You became a bur.
> You are annoying us.
> It is said about a person who makes a pest of himself.

The bald man doesn't have fleas.
> You can't take what a person doesn't have.

He became a gnat with drunkenness.
> He is very drunk.
> He is drunk as a skunk.

Even the ant has bile, and the fly a spleen.
> It is said about unlucky people who always have to pay the price no matter what.

Even that ant, with its iron rod, weighs forty pounds.
> A person finds himself capable according to his own judgment.

I see you as a mosquito.
> I am not taking you into consideration.
> I am not bothered by your presence.
> You are insignificant to me.

The black widow ate you.
> A great disaster found you.
> Your enemies succeed in harming you and bringing you down.

A termite is chewing at him.
> He is tormented by a silent worry.

He has been touched by a fly.
> A very thin-skinned person who takes offense at the slightest provocation.

Whoever has the fly gets stung by it.
> If the shoe fits, wear it.
> The guilty dog barks louder.

Not even a flea in his bosom.

 I wouldn't like to be in his place for anything in the world.

He is looking for fleas in the hay.

 He is looking for a needle in a haystack.

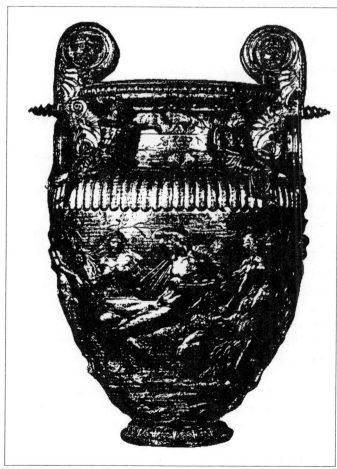

Bronze crater of Derveni, 4th century BC

REPTILES

He dragged the snake out from the hole.
>He put a bell on the cat.
>He pulled the chestnuts from the fire.
>He took over the hard task and had results.
>He had success over a hard situation.

May the snake that doesn't harm live a thousand years.
>An enemy that is not able to harm me is no enemy to me.

A snake cannot be made a friend.
>It is better to avoid the mean and cruel people who can harm us.
>It is hard to make friends with an enemy.

Don't warm a snake in your bosom.
>Never try to be nice to your enemy.

The sweet tongue is able to get the snake out from the hole.
>With kind words, all is possible.
>With gentleness and respect, we can conquer almost anything.

Even if a viper sings, it cannot become a canary.
>A bad and malicious person can sweet-talk all he wants; it doesn't make him a better person.

A double-faced friend is a coiled snake.
>An enemy is less dangerous than a bad friend who is closer to us and can harm us. A snake in the grass.

Don't step on the tail of a snake.
>Don't hurt your enemy because he is sure to find a way to bring greater harm to you.

As much charm as an eel has, that much bitterness a snake has.
>We say this when two people resemble each other physically, yet they have different personalities.

The bite of a snake hurts afterwards.
>Bad words and put-downs hurt after they've been said, and sometimes harm us in the long run.

Better for a snake's tongue to eat you than that of an evil woman.

The words of evil people hurt more than a snake-bite.

Shelter the snake in winter so it may bite you in the summer.

If you help an evil person in need, he will only harm you when he is better.

He spills his venom like a snake.

Gossipmongers can destroy people's lives.

A black snake ate you.

You were greatly hurt. A great sorrow found you.

Snakes girdled me.

I began to suspect danger.

I was alarmed. I was in a cold sweat.

If he spits on a snake it will burst.

It is said about a very angry person.

They made the crazy man drag the snake out from the hole.

This is said about people who make others take a risk on their account.

He is a tallies snake.

He is a deceiving person; a snake in the grass.

The Cycladic civilization was the first Aegean island civilization. Based on Milos and Thera (Santorini), Cycladic seafarers and traders conquered with their products all the harbours in the Aegean and Ionian Seas and opened up the sea route to the west before the Cretans, the Achaeans and the Phoenicians, reaching the shores of Italy and Spain.

ANIMALS

What did the fox want at the bazaar?
Clever people do not involve themselves in dangerous situations, they know how to avoid them.

Neither a cat, nor any damage.
Everything is fine.
We had no trouble, or any expenses.
A nice cover up after a bad situation.

One hundred years old is the fox, and one hundred-ten is her litter.
This refers to the audacity that the young show to their elders.
To be older doesn't necessarily mean you are wiser.

An angelic voice from a donkey's mouth.
It is said about the bad mannered and rude person who may talk sweetly in order to sway us in his plans.

Never accuse a horse that you have never mounted.
Never accuse or bad-mouth people that you don't really know, and never believe what others may tell you about such people.
What they say may not be true.

The lamb is used to having its wool taken.
Some people are used to misery and exploitation.

In her mind, a fox can cook roosters.
We think about and desire things we need or want.

They owed us, and they took our ox.
It is said about inconsiderate people who show no gratitude for the help we may have offered them.

Two donkeys were quarreling in a stranger's barn.
It is said when we find ourselves arguing about things that do not directly concern us.

They promised us hares with precious stones.
>Exaggerated and unrealistic promises.
>When someone promises many things, yet delivers nothing.
>This is said for someone who promises the impossible.

The fox and her kids make for one skin.
>When parents and their children are cunning.
>This is said about those subordinates who flatter their superiors.

Instead of a hare, he extracted a bear.
>Although we were waiting for something good, something awful happened.
>Even though we were trying for the best, we achieved the worst.

From galloping on a horse, he now rides on a donkey.
>When a person loses his position in a job, or in society.
>A sarcastic remark for someone who deserves to be demoted or put in his right place. Usually it refers to an arrogant person.

Let the donkey that cannot harm you, yell.
>If a person cannot harm you in any way, let him say whatever he wants about you.

What the fox cannot reach she makes into hangers.
>When we make excuses and down-play what we are not able to do. Sour grapes.
>When we scorn something only because we cannot have it.

They placed the wolf to guard of the sheep.
>When the wrong person is in the wrong place.
>When a person is given the wrong responsibilities.

No matter how much weight an ox may lose, it still makes up one whole ox.
>No matter what happens, a smart and capable person is always smart and capable.

Dogs come and grind it all, and don't give up any grain.
>Come and mess everything up, and don't pay attention to anybody.
>This is said in jest when someone messes things up.

When the cat leaves the hole the mouse plays the alphabet.
> When the person in charge is gone, the rest of the people manage to cause trouble.
> When the boss leaves, the employees do what they want.
> When the cat's away the mice will play.

A wolf never steals a lamb from his neighborhood.
> Most people act nice in their environment out of a sense of responsibility, or ulterior motive.

All pigs have the same snout.
> All swindlers have the same personality and motives.

Better to tie the donkey down than to go looking for it.
> It is wise to save what we have in case of an emergency.
> Safe bind, safe find.
> Prevention is better than cure.

He acted like a duck.
> He acted like he didn't know what was going on.
> He acted innocent.

Like a wet cat.
> A person who is caught red-handed.
> It is said in jest about a person who has failed at something and feels guilty about it.

A dog with fleas wants to find its mate.
> A miserable and disturbed person wants to find his equal.

The good lamb nurses from two mothers.
> A good and smart person has great success in life.

If the donkey doesn't kick, they don't take the load off its back.
> Protests bring results.
> If you don't ask for what you want, you'll never get it.

The pie is good and the dog is full.
> It is said about a capable person that does his job well without encroaching on the rights of others.

The person that hunts after two hares doesn't even get one.

The person who gets involved with many things ends up accomplishing nothing.

Don't tie a donkey in a horse's place.

Don't place a person with limited qualifications in a high position.

From one lamb you cannot get two hides.

We can't do two things at once.

You only profit once from any given situation.

A shitting bull will shit on all animals.

A bad example can entice us all.

A bad and incapable leaders can lead his troops to disaster.

I shitted on his donkey.

I told him off.

I cursed him out.

I put him in his place.

They offered him a donkey and he was looking at the teeth.

We are offered something of value, and we are concerned with minor details. Don't look a gift horse in the mouth.

Does the donkey fly? Indeed it flies.

When you are forced to accept what you are told.

When it is not in your advantage to disagree.

One, but a lion!

There's only one person for the job, but he's worthy, capable and wise.

You found a village without a dog and you walk around with a club.

It is said about the person who does what he wants and doesn't allow anything to get in his way.

A dog cannot become a lamb.

An evil person doesn't produce kind offspring.

We don't get good deeds from evil people.

When a fox grows old, he becomes the mascot of the dogs.
> When a fierce person grows old and loses his strength and capabilities, he may be ridiculed by others.

The camel doesn't notice her own hump, but she notices the hump of the others.
> It is said about people who don't admit their own faults but talk about the faults of others.

The eyes of a hare are different from the eyes of an owl.
> No matter how much we try to hide our true personality, it will surface.

He has the bone of a bat.
> It is said about a likable person, one sociable and congenial.

Better to lose the wool than the lamb.
> We would rather suffer a loss of minor significance than a loss of great importance.

We had a dog and it helped the wolf.
> It is said about a friend that betrays us.
> It is also said about shady lawyers.

When a fox grows old, she becomes a nun.
> When a cunning person grows old, he calms down because he can't be as active.

Green horses.
> Opposite things that can never be actualized.
> It is said about impossible things.

Hungry dogs tear down ovens.
> Sometimes, poverty-stricken or suppressed people cause trouble.

The good lamb is not separated from the herd.
> Good people are not banned from a team, or from society.

The hare emerges from the bush when you least expect it.
> Suddenly, happiness and profit come from unexpected sources.

When you see the footprints of a wolf, keep your eyes on the sheep.
>There is always some hint of danger or failure.
>There cannot be a criminal without a crime.

The wolf doesn't eat the counted sheep.
>When we are careful, we never lose.

A hungry bear doesn't dance.
>A hungry person has no desire to work, nor does he produce as he should. For a worker to produce, he must get paid.
>Work without rewards is ineffective.

A dog that barks doesn't bite.
>Many people may create a fuss with words, but are really harmless.

Speaking of the donkey.
>When we are talking about a person and he suddenly appears.
>Speaking of the devil.

Crocodile tears.
>It is said about a person who fakes crying in order to gain our pity.

He was rescued from the wolf's mouth.
>He was saved from sure death.
>He was saved from catastrophe.

Bulls are tied by the horns, a person is tied by his word.
>A worthy person keeps his word and thus gains respect and trust from others.

The mouse didn't fit in his hole, and yet he dragged a pumpkin.
>It is said about a poor person who, despite his poverty, puts himself at great expense.

A golden donkey is still a donkey.
>How we look isn't everything; our personality counts more.
>Looks can deceive.

An old donkey can't walk on a new path.
>We shouldn't wait for evil and mean people to change their personality. People will always act the way they are used to.

The person that acts like a lion at a time of peace becomes a roebuck when war sets in.
>It is said about a person who tries to avoid fighting in a war. The strength of a person can be utilized better at times of peace and not war.

By the time water reaches the reservoir, the frog will die.
>We have to help when the need arises. Offer your help when help is needed most.

If the camel didn't kneel, they would have never mounted him.
>We invite trouble when we submit.
>People who do not want responsibility should not accept positions of responsibility.

Funny faced bear with wide feet.
>It is said about the ugly woman, who may have a cunning heart and great wisdom.

A fox never falls in the same trap twice.
>The clever and cunning person never makes the same mistake twice.

The mouse is fine in it's hole.
>We are all at ease in familiar surroundings.

The hare was shaking the bush and brought trouble to himself.
>Sometimes, we show our enemies ways to harm us.
>Sometimes, out of stupidity, we are exposed with embarrassment in our environment.

The good horse merits its barley.
>The capable and hard-working person does a job well and profits from it.

He's proceeding like a turtle.
> He's going very slowly and taking his time in whatever he does.
> He is lazy in his tasks and responsibilities.

A sleeping cat doesn't catch mice.
> The person who is not focused or crazy doesn't succeed in life.
> You have to work to earn a living.

The hare is dragging the lion by a golden leash.
> It is said about a cunning wife, who, through sweet manipulations, is able to boss her husband.

If we all wore golden velvets, who would tend the donkeys?
> If we all act like the boss, who will get the job done?
> We all want pleasure, but who will work to secure our job and responsibilities?

We have eaten the donkey; only its tail is left.
> Let's not give up now that most of the work is done.

The person that sleeps with dogs wakes up with fleas.
> We may be influenced by the bad company we keep.

Like a cat and dog.
> We say this about two people who are constantly fighting and bickering with each other. Opposite traits between a couple.

The one who endures can manage a wolf.
> The person who perseveres succeeds at whatever he does in life.

Spurs are not needed for the horse that runs.
> A capable and ambitious person doesn't need to be urged to get the job done.

The frog is angry and the pond doesn't know it.
> Sometimes, we conceal bad feelings from people close to us.

He doesn't know how to split the hay between two donkeys.
> It is said about incapable and stupid people.

The fox is not satisfied with locusts.
> It is said about people who are not satisfied with small profits.
> These people are usually cunning and swindlers.

A fox is cunning, but the one that traps her is smarter.
> Sometimes, swindlers come across a person who outsmarts them.

The camel doesn't limp from the ear.
> It is said about minor damages that a wealthy person may endure.
> Minor damages cannot make a big business shut down.

The person that plays with the donkey will get kicked.
(The person who falls in the chicken feed will get pecked by the hens.)
> If we hang around bad people, we will get mistreated.
> If we involve ourselves in insignificant matters, we will take the
> blame in the end.

When the fox is hungry, she acts like she's sleeping.
> A cunning person tries to outsmart people by acting nice.

Never wake up a sleeping lion.
> Don't entice or provoke a fight with a person who can
> overpower you.

Even though the wolf grew old and shed his coat, he changed neither his good sense nor his mind.
> The wolf sheds his coat once a year; his disposition, never.
> Once a thief, always a thief.

He finished like a dog in a vineyard.
> He died a dog's death.

The sly fox is caught by its four legs.
> Deception always surfaces.

They hit the saddle so that the donkey will hear.
> This is said when people want to give a subtle hint.

The donkey suffers one way, the donkey rider another.
> When two people who work or live together don't seem to agree
> on things.

I tell it to my dog and the dog tells it to its tail.
Pass the buck. People who avoid responsibilities.

He became angry as a dog.
He is fuming with rage. He flew into a rage.

He has the patience of a donkey.
This is said about a very patient and enduring person who has the patience of a saint.

Greece is divided traditionally into ten geographical unities. The capital area, the Aegean Islands, Central Greece, Crete, Epirus, the Ionian Islands, Macedonia, the Peloponnese, Thessaly and Thrace. Athens is the capital of Greece where Acropolis, the city's and the country's "trade mark," is found.

RELIGION

The priest blesses his own whiskers first.
>Every clever person places his needs first.

He has nothing sacred or holy.
>When a person is rough and can't be trusted.
>When a person goes after what he wants and doesn't allow anything to get in his way. A very inconsiderate and selfish person.

Love the living and don't worry about memorializing the dead.
>Our actions count greater than our words.

God has blessed him with both hands.
>It is said about a very lucky and happy person.

The monk called the fish beans and ate them for lent.
>Sometimes, we make certain things into what they are not by their nature to suit our purpose.
>Some people make excuses to justify their actions.

He's the devil's sock.
>It is said about a smart, clever and capable person.

A sick man and a traveler have no sin.
>We should not lose our temper with the sick and the tired.

That's another priest's bible.
>It's a different story, or a different point of view.
>It's an entirely different situation.

Don't pay homage to a saint who doesn't help you.
>It is useless to pamper and please a person who doesn't want to help you.

From Ana to Kaiafas.
>From bad to worse. From one downfall to the next.

Even if you're a priest, you'll go in turn.
>No matter who we are, and what we have, we must wait our turn.
>It is said about an impatient person.

A crazy priest baptized you.
>It is said to a wild and crazy person.

It's from the devil's mother.
>It is said about something that is foreign and strange.

A person's gift, compared to a gift from God, is nothing.
>Only the things that God can give us, such as health, love, etc., are of any real value.

Not every day is Easter Sunday.
>We can't expect life to be fun and games all the time.
>We have to face all hardships that come our way.

The priest blesses the one he sees.
>We are more likely to help the people with whom we have more contact.

Who saw God and did not fear Him?
>It is said to describe a very angry man or a very frightful event.

Even the priest can grow tired of all the "Lord save us."
(Too much 'kyrie eleison' bores even God.)
>Constant nuisances and pleadings can agitate even the most patient person.

Star of Vergina

The lord rose.
>Everything went completely out of control. Chaos spread.

The priest is here and his robes are there.
>It is said about a very disorderly and messy person.

From your mouth to God's ear.
>May your wish be granted and come true.
>I hope what you say comes trues.

Monkhood is hard.
>It is said about a very difficult situation or undertaking that is almost impossible to accomplish.

From Noah's time.
>It is something very old.

The imposing appearance of a bishop and the heart of a miller.
>It is said about a person who has a very attractive appearance, yet has a very shallow personality with poor sentiments.
>Judge not according to the appearance.
>Don't judge a book by its cover.

The robes do not make the priest.
>The appearance of a person can be deceiving.
>A person's personality and abilities should carry more weight on our impression.

He changes hymns.
>When a person is insisting on one thing, then suddenly changes the story and insists on something totally different.
>It is said to note a change in someone's attitude.

God nourishes the birds, but He doesn't put the food in their mouths.
>We shouldn't expect everything to come to us from God.
>We have to "get and chew our own food."

God loves the thief, but He also loves the homeowner.
>God loves everybody, but he takes better care of the virtuous and good-natured man. Honesty is always rewarded.

The devil has no goats, yet he was selling cheese.

It is said about the cunning and swindling ways of certain people. It can also be said when a person lacks the means and the ability to do a certain thing, yet he tries to fool others into believing that he can do it. It is usually said about merchants.

A short psalm, hallelujah.

There's no need for many words. Get to your point.

The devil is destroying his nest.

When a thief or swindler ends his business.

If you don't give, you won't be sanctified.

Charity is a good thing.

When we give to those in need, we feel much better about ourselves.

The monk was angered and he burned his robes.

Anger always leads us to rash and foolish actions.

A person's anger can harm himself.

Alone, not even in Paradise.

Loneliness can sometimes be unbearable, regardless of all the possessions we may have.

God knows which tree to wilt.

God knows whom to punish.

Do a good deed for a poor man and you will find it from God.

Charity is always rewarded.

Wide sleeves are good, but they are worn by the bishops.

It is said in jest about people who claim to be more than what they really are.

Many desire honors and praise, but few are truly worthy.

May the Archbishop love me, even if the deacons hate me.

As long as the tough boss likes me, I don't care if the others dislike me.

You are holding a memorial with another man's boiled wheat.
> It is said about people who act like big shots with somebody else's money. To ride on somebody else's wings.

The devil broke his leg.
> After all the misfortune we had, happiness came unexpected.

I want to become a monk to save my soul, but the devil I have in my pants won't allow me.
> This notes the sexual temptations we experience that can stand in the way of living a virtuous life.

Never promise a candle to a saint or a doughnut to a child.
> We must be sure we can keep our promises.

On horseback they go to church, on horseback they kiss the icons.
> It is said about the very rich, the very powerful people, whose riding on a horse sets them apart from the common people.

Don't even tell the priest.
> It is said when a person is saved from a major catastrophe, when he had lost all hope.

He doesn't even offer adulation to his angel.
> It is said about a cheap and thrifty person.

The devil grew old and became a monk.
> It is said about the reckless youth who grows up to be a wise and respected man.

The monk had nothing else to do but fight with the flies.
> It is said about the lazy who don't know what to do and thus involve themselves with trivialities.

I saw many things, but never a gypsy priest.
> It is said about something totally unbelievable.

The lame, the blind, all rush to St. Pandeleimon.
> It seems that all lazy people hang out in the same place.

Since we saw a crazy priest, we've been chanting all day.
> Workers do not care to produce when the foreman is an idiot.

God willing, and time allowing.
> We say this when we want to wish that no obstacle stands in the way of achieving or getting what we want.

Don't judge, so that you won't be judged.
> We shouldn't judge others if we don't want to be the center of gossip ourselves.

Even the saint needs to be threatened.
> Sometimes, we have to stand up even to those higher than ourselves in order to get what we want and what we need.

I made him God and saint.
> I begged him to help me.

To the saint we light one candle, and to the devil two.
> It is said about a person who is obviously master minding and plotting to do no good.

They have him in the devil's ledger.
> They have the worst possible opinion about him.
> They are plotting against him.

When God gives the flour, the devil takes the sack.
> Sometimes, bad luck stands in our way of enjoying what we worked for.

Each one in his own home and God in all.
> Each for himself and God for all.

God delays but doesn't forget.
> The proper and just punishment will come eventually.
> The guilty will not escape retribution.

The voice of the mob, the wrath of god.
> Man proposes, but God disposes.

There are twelve Apostles, and each one wept about his own suffering.

Every man is wrapped up in his own concerns and problems.

*Thessaloniki, the true capital of Macedonia
and the cultural capital of Europe.*

HOME AND LIFE IN GENERAL

If you don't praise your own house, it will fall and crush you.
> The person who puts down his family hurts himself in the end.
> Prudent is the man who take pride in his own household.

Home, my little home, my poor little shack.
> No matter how small or poor, we think our home is the best
> there is. No matter how poor our family is, we consider it better
> than the others. A man's home is his castle.

Our house is small, yet our stomach is big.
> We may be poor, but our hospitality is great.

He who controls his house also controls his life.
> The person who runs a good household can manage this life well.

When God pairs up two bad people, He ruins two houses.
> Failed marriages usually effect the families of the couple as well.

Every person is king in his house.
> We all feel more comfortable in our home, or in our familiar
> environment.

Every house is my home, and every yard belongs to me.
> We say this about people who are never satisfied with anything.
> It is also said about the person that feels comfortable no matter
> where he is.

Even the bricks laugh at the person who sells his home.
> It is foolish for a person to sell his home for purely monetary gain.

If you are respected in your home, you are respected by your neighbors.
> If you are respected by the members of your family, your
> neighbors are more likely to respect you as well.

I'd rather have olives and hard bread in my house than sugar in a stranger's house and be told what to do.
> I'd rather be poor in my house than rich in someone else's house.
> This was said about women who work as maids for the rich.

I hold my lock and somebody else holds my hut.
> When we don't seem to understand the evil that someone is doing to us.
> When we think everything is fine, yet behind our back our enemies are plotting.

Small cooking makes greater homes.
> Saving money always has its benefits.
> When we control our expenses, we are able to save more money.

He has it as a double swinging door.
> When someone has many chances and breaks in life.
> When a person is able to function in many different ways.
> Run with the hare and hunt with the hounds.

When the house is but cinders, everybody brings water.
> When the damage is already done, people try to help.

Like a gypsy's tent.
> It is said about a very messy house.
> A house that resembles a pigsty.

You're the fragrance of the house.
> You are the foundation of the house. It is usually said about the strongest, or smartest person in the family. A person who is the pride and joy of his family.

Not a door without a nail, and not a house with shame.
> Every family has its share of faults.

> The most brilliant Aegean island civilization is the Cretan, or Minoan civilization, which flourished in Crete mainly in the 3rd and 2nd millenia BC and took its name from the legendary king of Knossos, Minos. In 1450 BC, Crete had become a mighty sea power and had amassed great riches and treasures which allowed it to build, between 2200 and 1550 BC, the renowned Cretan palaces of Knossos and Phaestos, where the arts flourished.

NAMES

Philip found Nathaniel.
>It is said when two people get along well.

Sometimes John is not well, sometimes his ass hurts.
>It is said about people who are constantly complaining about
>their health.
>A hypochondriac person.

Does it matter if it's John or Johnny?
>It's the same thing.

Wherever there's a John, there's silver.
>It is said about people who are impressionable and can be taken
>advantage of.

What's wrong John? What was always wrong.
>From what does an idiot suffer? From stupidity.

John treats and John drinks.
>When a person spends his money on himself.

We like what John has, but we dislike John.
>When we admire certain traits a person has, yet we don't care
>much for the person.

Whatever is known by Constantine is not known by anybody.
>Sometimes we think a person is stupid, yet he may know more
>than anyone else.

Let me burn you, John, and I'll spread honey on you.
>When we try to do something nice for a person after we did
>something wrong to hurt him.

It was brought by the devil and by Michael's hood.
>When coincidences and bad luck collide, causing misfortune.

The earth is being destroyed, and Mary is looking in the mirror.
>It is said about careless and selfish people who do what they
>want despite the bad things that are happening around them.

Emanuel has changed clothes and put his cap on backwards.
When a situation appears to have changed but in reality stays the same. That's old wine in a new bottle.

Forty five men named John, with the mentality of one rooster.
A put down on men whose name is John.

How are you John? I am sowing fava beans.
This is said to express lack of communication.

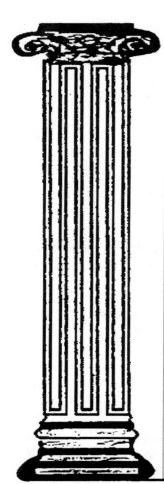

In around 2000 BC, the Achaeans appeared on the stage of history. More powerful and better armed, and using horses and war chariots, they prevailed over the entire region starting from Thessaly and ending in the Peloponnese. Their language also prevailed over the whole of Greece and they absorbed many elements of the Cretan and Aegean civilizations. A consequence of this odd mixture was the creation of a superior civilization, the Creto-Mycenaean. The Achaeans imposed themselves in the Mediterranean, developing trade with Asia Minor, Egypt, Lower Italy and Spain. They established permanent installations in Cyprus and in Rhodes. Their products were much in demand. Mycenae, the most important Achaean center, reached its peak around 1600 BC, during the Bronze Age. Naturally fortified and strategically placed, Mycenae quickly became very powerful. Homer described it as "golden Mycenae" because of the gold transported there by the Achaeans from the Pharaohs of Egypt. In 12th century BC the Mycanaean civilization was obliterated by internal conflict and in 1100 BC by the invasion of the Dorians.

BIRDS

The bird flew.

When we lose a good opportunity because we didn't act quickly enough. You missed your chance.

The cuckoo cost him the price of a nightingale.

When a person is put at great expense and profits very little. When we pay through the nose.

An innocent dove.

It is said in jest of a person who is acting innocent.

One swallow doesn't bring spring.

One achievement is not enough for us to reach our goals.

He killed the goose that lay the golden eggs.

When a person unwisely destroys his benefactor.
It is said about a greedy person who wants everything at once.

The cluckings are heard over there, but the hens lay their eggs somewhere else.

Sometimes we are fooled by the appearance of things.
When promise is seen in one place, yet profit is found somewhere else.

He has no nest, he has no egg.
> The person that has no place to live, or a family, has a hard time making it in life.
> When a person doesn't have a steady job, he cannot succeed.

With one bullet, two turtle-doves.
> When we try one thing, and succeed at two.
> To kill two birds with one stone.

Where many roosters crow, dawn is slow in appearing.
> When there's a lot of commotion and many opinions, a good decision is almost impossible to be made.
> Too many cooks spoil the broth.

The female bird makes the nest.
> The woman is the one who sets up the home and takes care of the family.

Every rooster crows in his own yard.
> We all feel more comfortable at home, or in our own environment, where we can produce the most.

He loaded it all on the rooster.
> When a person abandons a task because of laziness and bad planning.
> It is also said when somebody fails his exams due to lack of preparation.

Before the eggs hatched, he was counting the chickens.
> It is said about impatience in gaining profit.
> It is said about the calculations and plans we make based on the profits we anticipate.

The old hen has the broth.
> An older lady carries more intrigue because she has more knowledge and experience.
> Quality improves with age.

I have no hens, nor do I fight with the fox.
> It is said when a person has no dealings with others, nor does he give reason for others to fight with him.

He was left like a cuckoo.

It is said about a person left alone, high and dry.

From a crow's mouth, "crow" you'll hear.

From bad mannered and rough people, you'll only hear negative and bad things.

The cage is silver, but it's holding an owl.

It is said about a person with an attractive appearance, but a bad personality.

When a situation looks good, but is in fact of no use or profit.

Even his rooster lays eggs.

We say this about a very lucky and successful person.

The donkey called the rooster "fathead".

This is said about people who overlook their own faults and criticize others.

The pot calling the kettle black.

When a chicken drinks water, she lifts her head and sees God.

We should always thank God for every fortune, however small, in our lives.

Better a sparrow in my hand than an eagle in the air.

It is better to possess things of lesser value than to go after things of higher value but less certainty.

"Better five birds in hand than ten in the bush. . ."

A crow will not peck the eye of another crow.

People with similar interests tend to protect each other.

My hen, sit on your eggs, so your chickens may hatch.

We need to have patience and responsibility in order to achieve our goals.

With patience and determination we fulfill our goals in life.

They find the partridge's nest from its voice.

Sometimes, we give away family secrets and personal information in the course of gossiping.

The delicious apple is eaten by the crow.
> It is said about certain unworthy men who marry desirable and worthy women.

In trying to learn the walk of the partridge, the rook forgot its own.
> Those who try to imitate the acts of their superiors forget or neglect their own attributes.

If only the rook had any knowledge to offer you.
> A derogatory remark about people of low intelligence.

The good bird chirps from its egg.
> A good, capable and worthy person is noticed early in life.

The eagle chases big birds.
> A brave and proud person doesn't bother with people of inferior status.

The smart bird is caught by its beak.
> Sometimes, even smart and clever people can be outsmarted.

Better a bird on a branch than a bird in a cage.
> It is said about those who prefer to remain unmarried.

He has the knowledge of a rooster.
> It is said about a person of low intelligence who is not able to perform the simplest of tasks.

When a crow becomes white and turns into a dove.
> It is said about something that cannot be done because it is impossible by nature.
> "When hell freezes over."

I became a partridge.
> I became well.
> I am healthy.

The hen pokes her eye out while she's digging.
> It is said for a person who brings about misery unto himself.
> A self-destructive person.

He's a horned owl.

> He is a real idiot, a stupid person.

A sly bird is caught by its own two feet.

> A cunning person outsmarts none.

The wicked bird may temporarily triumph but does not win.

> Evil never conquers.
> Evil may win the battle, but never the war.

All the birds migrate, and the sparrows stay behind.

> Size does not measure perseverance.

He has the proud air of a peacock and calls for ram's milk.

> This is said about a pretentious person with unrealistic demands.

A bird in the hand is worth two in a bush.

> Don't take any chances about something you are not sure of.

CLOTHES

He wore his pants as a turban.
>Because of his behavior, he became a spectacle.
>It is said when a person acts in an inexcusable and foolish manner.

A shoe from your native land, even if it has been patched.
>Marry a woman from your native place, even if she's not perfect or wealthy.
>Do not look at things that are far, neglecting what is near.

They put his two feet in one shoe.
>They forced him to do something. They cornered him.

He put a fez on us.
>It is said about a person that leaves his debts unpaid.

Sew and tear, so you'll have work to do.
>When a person keeps busy for no apparent reason or gain.

He took his wet clothes and left.
>He left in embarrassment.

He doesn't have pants on his ass.
>He is poor. He is needy.

He cut his sleeve to patch up his pants.
>It is said about people who live in great poverty.

The mindless man wore pants, and was looking at every step he took.
>It is said about a person who has unexpected success and is proud of it.

Starting from March a shirt, and from August a wool sweater.
>The clothes we wear depend on the weather. When summer approaches we wear light clothing, and as winter comes, we wear heavier clothing.

Take off your cap and hit me.
>It is said about a person who has many faults, but puts down others.

He wore his hat crooked.
> He managed just fine.
> He was successful.

Alexandra's buttons.
> The crux of the matter.
> An obstacle, difficulty, or source of irritation.

I kissed and pissed on aprons.
> I made a fool of myself and I begged to get what I wanted.
> I humiliated myself in order to get what I was after.

It came to him like a glove.
> He deserved what he got.
> It suited him fine.

He's tearing up his clothes.
> He is frustrated.
> He is out of control.

I have handed him his shoes.
> I fired him.
> I ended our relationship.

You've become a tight corset.
> You're annoying.

I don't know where his cap is from.
> He's stranger. I have no idea where he's from.

He appeared all buttoned-up.
> He looked rather non-committal.
> He did not want to get involved.

What do I owe him? For the wool, or for the tailoring?
> I owe him nothing at all.

He came out of his clothes.
> He was mad.
> He was frustrated.

His cap is full of demons.
> It is said about an extremely smart, clever, and capable person.

I have numerous stitches for your fur coat.
> I have many reason to quarrel with you.
> This saying emphasizes reason for holding a grudge.

You're not my fur coat's sleeve.
> You have no business with me.

He was left with fabric to fabric.
> He has no money left; empty pockets.
> He became poor.

When a tailor cuts wool, he cuts his own suit first.
> Personal gain comes first.

Clothing for the world, and food for our appetite.
> We should dress according to fashion, we should eat according to our appetite.

Their dirty laundry came out on the street.
> Their personal business became public knowledge.

You write us off on your old shoes.
> You don't care about us.
> You don't take into consideration our feelings and views.

It's a big sleeve.
> It is a big burden.
> It's a difficult situation.

He is a long sleeve.
> It is said about a philanderer who does not discriminate in his sexual relationships with women.

Whoever guards his clothes has half of them saved.
> Put safety first in whatever you do.
> Do not overextend yourself.

He fights with his own clothes.
> He quarrels with anything and everything near him.
> It is said about a very quarrelsome person.

He is on the rag.
> It is said about a person who is like a bear with a sore hand.
> He is in a bad mood.

An idle person has nothing to do so he ties and unties his breaches.
> An idle person is a useless person.

The thread follows the needle.
> The results of your deeds stay with you forever; or, children take after their parents.

They became ass and underpants.
> They became inseparable. They are hand in glove.
> They are two peas in a pod.

She stuffed him into her underpants.
> It is said about manipulative women who lead men by the nose.

FAMILY AND RELATIVES

The more our mother-in-law drinks, the kinder she greets us.
> Wine can bring on merry spirits and sentiments, even to the most annoying and miserable person.

The good mother's first child is a girl.
> This expresses every mother's wish to have a girl for company and comradery in life.

My aunt says one thing, and my ears hear something different.
> Bad communication between people.

Have a parent's blessing, and you can even climb a mountain.
> Always obey your parents in order to succeed in life.

From all the fragrances, mother smells the best.
From all the women, mother is the greatest.

Our mother knows how to bake a pie but only when she has flour.
This saying notes economic hardships a family may experience. Although the mother is able to make the most delicious pie, she can't because she cannot afford the ingredients.

A mother-in-law's nagging is an unbearable evil.
A mother-in-law's nagging is nerve wrecking.
An unfair reputation attributed to mothers-in-law.

If they didn't hit it off, they wouldn't have become in-laws.
It is said when two people or two families get along.

Two brothers were fighting, and two crazy people were happy.
Only stupid people enjoy when two siblings fight with each other.

If you don't respect your parents, who will respect you?
The person who respects his parents is respected by his friends and family.

If the baby doesn't cry, his mother won't feed it.
If you don't ask for what you want, you will never get it.
If you don't take care of your own matters, you will not succeed.

The peevish mother-in-law forgets that she was once a bride.
We must always remember what we went through, and not bother other people for no apparent reason.

The baby was not even born and they bought a cap for it.
We should not rush into things before the proper time comes.

My child's child is twice my child.
It is said about grandparents who love their grandchildren a great deal.

United siblings, happy homes.
A loving family is a basis for happiness and social status.

The child was losing its mother and the mother was losing her child.
> It is said when things get out of control, or when there's a lot of commotion and confusion.

The blessing of parents builds palaces.
> When we have our parent's blessing, we can overcome all difficulties in life with greater ease.

My brother and I, against my cousin, and the three of us, against a stranger.
> Family alliances.
> A united family against a hostile foe.

Love you brother, and not your share.
> Love your brother, and don't let the thought of economic profit get in your way.

With your relative, eat, drink, but don't start any business.
> It is better to have a good time with relatives than to go into business with them.

May there be no bickering between a couple, or a fight among siblings.
> Siblings should always be loving to each other.

The brother is far away, but close is the neighbor.
> Sometimes we can count more on friends and neighbors than on relatives.

Even if a mother-in-law is made of sugar, she is always bitter.
> No matter how nice a mother-in-law may be, she is still a mother-in-law.

Listen to your father and advise your son.
> We must listen to our parents and take into account what they tell us because they have more experience and knowledge than we do, and in turn, we must advise and look after our own children and pass on what we learn from our parents.

THE BODY

All fingers are not the same.
> We are not all the same. Not every situation is the same.

The tongue forgets and tells the truth.
> Sometimes the truth slips through words.

You grabbed the bald man by his hair.
> It is said when we seek profit from where it just doesn't exist.
> Things that can't be actualized.

The person who cries over others' worries loses his eyes.
> The person who gets all worked up over another person's
> business may come out to be the bad guy in the end.

Whichever finger you cut off, it hurts just the same.
> It is said about the mother that loves all her children equally.

If you can see the nape of your neck, then you'll see me.
> You'll never see me again.

What the knife cuts can be healed, what the tongue cuts, cannot.
> Sometimes we can create immeasurable harm with our words.
> Sometimes bad words hurt more than a knife.

They went for wool, and came out with a haircut.
> It is said when a sure thing falls through.
> The biter, the bitten.

The tongue a shoe, but the mind, a pit.
> It is said about a chattering person who always speaks nonsense.

I didn't smell my fingers.
> We say this when we don't know something, or we could not
> guess that something was going to happen.

The heart's key is held by the word.
> We influence people's emotions with our words.

One hand washes the other, and both wash the face.
> Mutual respect, cooperation and honor lead to success.
> If you'll scratch my back, I'll scratch yours.

His eye turned black.
> It is said about a person in despair who has no luck, or is poor.

Everyone's ass is farting, but from mine, not a sound.
> This saying expresses grievance.
> Everybody is talking stupidities, and I am not able to say a word.

The heart doesn't always smile when the face does.
> Sometimes, we have to pretend we are happy, even though we are sad or upset.

Better for my eye to fall out than my name.
> This saying notes the importance of having a good name in society.
> Better to lose an eye than your reputation.

A tongue has no bones, yet it breaks bones.
> With words we can accomplish many things. We can easily put down people.
> The devastating results of gossip; words cut more than swords.

Extend your legs as far your quilt reaches.
> Our demands should be in line with our abilities.
> Live within your means.

Don't sever the finger that points the way.
> Don't be ungrateful.
> Don't bother the person who has helped you.
> Don't bite the hand that feeds you.

Muff your ears if you want them to feed you.
> The person who is in need of other people's help should be cooperative and grateful.

Kiss the hand that you cannot bite.
> We have to adjust to every situation we encounter. If we can't assume authority over a matter, we should use wiser ways, such as respect and compliments, to get what we want.

The walls have ears, and the shrubs have eyes.
>Even if nobody's around, we should be careful not to reveal what we don't want others to know.

He sticks his nose everywhere.
>He gets involved in everything and becomes annoying.

Blood can never become water.
>No matter how much relatives fight, they make up, and still love each other.
>Blood is thicker than water.

The lengthening of the tongue, the hemming of the mind.
>Sometimes, talking too much makes a person appear stupid.

The deaf man grew ears, and the blind man, eyes.
>It is said about an idiot who finally realized what he can gain from a certain situation.

His hand is too short to reach me.
>He is incapable of harming me because I am better than him.

Every hair with its shade.
>Even the meek have their worth and place in society.

Even his ears are laughing.
>He is happy. He succeeded in what he wanted to do.

Spite can poke an eye out.
>Spite is one of the worst faults a person can have. It can create many problems and bring about great despair.

The tongue honors the face.
>The way a person speaks enhances him.

The person that holds his tongue saves his head.
>A modest and well-spoken person can never lose.

He remained with his finger in his mouth.
>When a person expected one thing and received something else.

We paid the hair of our heads.
> We paid a lot of money.

It is hard to pull a hair out of a bare chested man.
> From a poor person you can't get anything.
> Unreasonable expectations.

Why the face? We didn't call you a hunchback.
> Why are you upset? We didn't mean to hurt you.
> Don't be so sensitive.
> We didn't put you down.

Spit into your bosom.
> We say this to avoid the effects of the evil eye.

The one who has the beard also has the combs.
> The person who has the advantage over a situation also has the chance to manipulate profit.
> The one who is in control can tell others what to do.

His ear doesn't sweat.
> He has an indifferent, fearless, and intense personality.

Look at me with one eye, and I'll look at you with two.
> If you love me a little bit, I'll love you a great deal.
> If you watch out for me a little, I'll watch out for you more.

He left me in his foot.
> He left me in charge.

The one-eyed man ruled the blind.
> Those who have half the ability prevail over those who have no ability at all.

The crust fell from his face.
> He is no longer embarrassed.
> He has no more shame.

He has poison in his mouth.
> He expresses rudeness, and his words are out to hurt others.
> A gossip monger.

Your tongue became hairy.
>When a person talks too much.
>Your tongue wears thin.

They are hanging from his lips.
>They are paying very close attention to what he says.

Even if a fart doesn't smell, it's still a fart.
>Even if a negative word doesn't hurt us, it is still negative.

The clever man's ear is deaf.
>A smart person doesn't listen to idle gossip and empty words.

An ass that farts doesn't need a doctor.
>It is said in jest of the healthy that have no need of doctors.
>A healthy person doesn't need medical attention.

His stomach is playing the guitar.
>It is said about a hungry person.

Whoever has no mind, has feet.
>A stupid person, as well as a person who is not well informed, or
>illiterate, has to make double the effort to succeed at something.
>A person who uses his physical power and not his intellect.

He emerged white-faced.
>He was successful at something very difficult.
>He acted in the right way.

Eyes that are not seen, are quickly forgotten.
>When two people do not see each other for a long time, they
>forget about one another.

Everything is possible, but a hairless man's whiskers can not be pulled.
>It is said about things that are impossible to do.

He's pulling his hair.
>It is said when a person has failed and is very upset.

Many hands are blessed, and many mouths are cursed.
　　Action and deeds are better than words.

You can count them on your fingers.
　　When there is little of something.

Your eyes, fourteen!
　　Be very careful, stay on the alert!　Look out!
　　Keep your mind on it.

He took me with bad eye.
　　I got on his wrong side.

I throw ashes in his eyes.
　　I pull the wool over his eyes.

He eats her with his eyes.
　　He gazes wistfully at her.

She made my head into a cauldron.
　　She talked my head off.

My head is a cauldron.
　　My head is in a whirl.

In 776 BC, the olympic games were
inaugurated to honor Olympian Zeus.
Armistices were declared for their
duration.

FOOD AND DRINK

You haven't hatched from your egg yet!
> You haven't matured yet.

Whoever touches honey licks his fingers.
> The one who comes across valuables or money puts some in his pocket.

For others you hatch the egg, but you come to me clucking.
> You compliment me but you go spend your money elsewhere.
> When we simply hear words but gain no profit.

Sweet like honey, but heavy as salt.
> It is said about a good and capable person.

No butter can be made.
> It is said about a business proposal, or about a situation that is not profitable.

The one who drinks free wine gets drunk twice.
> We may abuse things that are for free.

You stepped on the pie.
> This is said about a person who has failed at something.

Strong vinegar pierces the bottle.
> It is said about a person with uncontrollable anger.

The two of you boil in the same cauldron.
> It is said about two people with a similar bad personality.
> It also can be said about two people who are interested in the same things.

When you have bread, you are wise.
> If you are wealthy, you can appear to be smart.

Boil rice.
> It is said about a misfortune.
> To hell with it.

Bean by bean the sack gets filled.
>With good economizing, a person can become wealthy and
>attain what he wants. "Little and often fills the purse."

The person that loves honey is not afraid of the bees.
>The person that loves passion and all of its benefits is able to
>withstand all the dangers.
>The person that loves money and all that comes with it is not
>afraid of the pains and dangers of trying to attain it.
>A passionate person is not afraid to take risks with sexual
>escapades.

Now that the sauce turned to yogurt, we have no spoon.
>It is said about our inability to exploit certain situations.
>It is also said about old men who can no longer make love,
>although they come across many chances to do so.

The neighbor's eggs are always larger.
>This saying expresses the jealousy we have towards others.
>We are never satisfied with what we have.
>The grass is greener on the other side.

He will make for us the golden egg.
>It is said sarcastically about a group of people who fuss over a
>person thinking they will greatly benefit from him in the end.

Pie, fall so I can eat you.
>It is said about the lazy person who wants everything served to
>him because he doesn't want to do it himself.

Few words are sugar and no words are honey.
>The person that doesn't talk a great deal can never lose.
>We can only create trouble and problems by saying too much.

The children of the wise cook before they're hungry.
>We should always plan ahead and we should always be prepared
>for everything.

You should earn your bread with the sweat of your brow.
>We should all work for what we need and for what we want.
>Without working, we can't accomplish anything.

The one who cooks knows what he's eating.
>The person that watches over his business knows exactly what is going on, and has less fear of being swindled by others.

There is a hole in the pea puree.
>They laid a trap for us.
>Something is not right.
>I smell a rat.
>There is a catch somewhere.

It came to him like candy.
>He found it useful.
>He got what he needed.

The thirsty man drinks in silence.
>A person in need doesn't create a fuss so he won't lose what he was already given.

Don't worry if the pie you are not eating burns.
>We should not get involved in situations that have nothing to do with us.
>Mind your own business.

He wants the toast soaked.
>This saying notes laziness.
>He wants everything on a plate.

He lost the eggs and the baskets.
>It is said when a person loses all he has.

This pie for that friend.
>We treat people according to their worth and social status.

We ate bread and salt.
>We share fond memories. We have endured hardship together.
>We've been very close with one another.

He ate the noodles.
>It is said when a person is disappointed in love.
>It is said when a person loves someone and is rejected.
>He got the mitten.

Are they shelling eggs for you?
>It is said to a person who is laughing for no apparent reason.

Cured meat is not afraid of salt.
>It is said about people who have been through a great deal of trouble and worries and are still able to endure more.

The well-fed person doesn't believe the hungry man.
>Wealthy people may have a hard time feeling compassion for the poor.

Bread cannot be made without yeast.
>In order to start any type of business, we must invest money.

Too many cooks spoil the broth.
>When we have many people voicing their views and opinions, a good and sound decision is hard to reach.

The month of honey.
>It refers to the first month of a marriage because, usually, a couple avoids fights or quarrels during the first month of their marriage.

We have no bread, yet the cat drags a pie.
>Sometimes, wealth is distributed unjustly.
>Sometimes, the ones who are in real need get no breaks, while others, who are not in need, get more.

Skill needs a skillman, while peas need oil.
>Every job needs to be done by the right person, like every food needs the right ingredient.

He bought it for a piece of bread.
>He bought it at a low price.

Give the egg a haircut and take the hair.
>It is said about severe poverty.

If the milk spills, it can't be gathered.
>We can't correct certain mistakes after they were made.
>Don't cry over spilled milk.

Empty walnuts cannot make a pie.
>Without any means do not expect profit and success.

May your pepper vanish, so I can see what you will achieve.
>It is said about people who depend heavily on patronage.

He carries wine and drinks water.
>It is said about a person who puts a great effort into something and is not properly rewarded.

He made him a product of salt.
>He beat him up black and blue.
>He made a fool out of him.

Sit on your eggs.
>Don't create any problems.
>Don't get involved in anything.
>Mind your business.

Hurry can bake the bread, but it doesn't bake it well.
>When we are in a hurry to get a job done, the result are not always great.
>Haste makes waste.

His tongue drips honey.
>He speaks nicely, and what he says is pleasant.

In a stranger's wine, don't add water.
>Look after your own business.
>Don't involve yourself in the affairs of others.

Words of the tin bowl.
>Words that we can't trust.
>Balderdash, idle talk, rumors.

Live till May to eat clover, and till August to taste the grapes.
>Do not put too much weight on grand promises others may give you, promises that very likely will not be fulfilled.

The one who has a lot of butter puts on his vegetables.
>The person who has a great deal of money can squander.

His talk has no salt.
> It is said when a person is a dull speaker and what he says is of no interest.

They became milk and honey.
> It is said about two people who make up after an argument.

The hungry person always dreams of loaves.
> It is said about things we want, but don't have; unfilled wishes or desires.

The longer you knead the dough, the more it rises.
> The more you care about your business, and the harder you work, the greater you success and profits will be.
> The more a person is educated, the better he becomes.

Chestnuts want wine and walnuts want honey.
> Every situation calls for the proper methods or skills.

Eat a big bite, but don't say a big word.
> Action matters more than words. Results are better than words.

He's the gallant youth of lentil soup.
> It is said about a person who brags about his abilities and courage, yet is in reality an incapable coward. A swash-buckler.

Eggs aren't dyed with farts.
> Poor means and abilities reflect poor results.

He took the secret out of the oven.
> He let the cat out of the bag.
> He blurt out the secrets.

He ate weed.
> He got a beating.

Hunger has no eyes.
> Beggars should not be choosers.

He is an old mess tin.
> He is an experienced man; an old hand.

FRUITS AND VEGETABLES

The pear has the tail behind.
> All the difficulties are at the end.
> The day of reckoning is yet to come.
> Expect difficulties to emerge at the end of a job or a situation.
> Don't consider anybody happy till the end.

He took the chestnuts out of the fire.
> We took over a difficult situation and made it work.
> He stuck his neck out.

The apple falls under the apple tree.
> It is said when the kids greatly resemble the parents.
> A chip off the old block.
> Like father, like son.

The inside of an olive, and the outside of a walnut.
> This is said when we are offered useless things.

An apple a day puts the doctor aside.
> This saying expresses the nutritious value of apples and all fruits and vegetables in our diet.

The figs, figs, and the trough, trough.
> Say it like it is.
> Say who is right and who is wrong.
> Call a spade a spade.

He made it pomegranate.
> He didn't treat the situation correctly and he failed.
> He made a mess.

Slowly and gradually, the unripe grape becomes sweet as honey.
> With the passing of time, our efforts pay off.
> Patience is a virtue. Everything comes to those who waits.

The good pears are eaten by the pigs.
> It is said when something good falls into bad hands.
> It is also said when beautiful and capable women end up with miserable men.

Every walnut tree's walnut.
> It is said about any gathering place where all sorts of people come together.

Garlic and water make the person strong.
> Sometimes, the less we put in the food, the better it is.
> The therapeutic properties of garlic and water in folk medicine.

The bitter eggplant isn't taken by hoarfrost.
> It is said about people who are used to misfortunes and can withstand anything.

Figs are soft, but they ruin the teeth.
> Certain things are very pleasurable, but they can also harm us.

Pumpkins on the ceiling.
> It is said about insignificant things and words.

Counted beans.
> When a situation is coming to an end.
> When we are running out of money.

Your command a cabbage, and your order a cucumber.
> I don't care about you.
> You are insignificant to me.

If you want to taste the sweetness of a date, give it to a poor person.
> Charity makes us feel better.

Better veggies with sweetness than sugar with bitterness.
> Better cabbage with peace than sugar with nagging.
> I'd rather be poor and happy, than rich and miserable.
> Better a little with contentment that much with contention.

We are not dividing chestnuts.
> We have to seriously try to accomplish what we want.

Dirty vegetables make a bad salad.
> From bad materials, don't expect a good product.
> From bad people, don't expect kind words and deeds.

They caught him in the leeks.
> The caught him in the act.

He stepped on the melon peel.
> They tricked him.
> He fell in the trap.

When you hear of many cherries, hold a small basket.
> When you hear many promises, don't expect a great deal to happen.

The lazy person doesn't eat almonds so he won't have to crack them.
> Because a lazy person doesn't want to strain himself, he sacrifices his own pleasures.
> The lazy person avoids work, even when he stands to greatly profit.

Two watermelons don't fit under one arm.
> We can't do two things at once. When we undertake many things, we have a hard time succeeding at one.

The tree is recognized by its fruit.
> People are judged by their actions.
> A business is valued by the profits.

Ares-mares-koukounares.
> This is said about something or someone who makes no sense.
> Balderdash, gibberish, nonsense.

Zucchini with oregano.
> It expresses disbelief in things said.
> You are talking nonsense.

What you plant you will harvest.
> As you sow so you'll reap.
> Man is responsible for what he does with his life.

The vineyard needs a vineyard keeper and a home needs a master.
> No house is good for anything without a good manager.

FISH

He's passing his time like a crab in a pot.
It is said about a person who is going through many problems.

They fried the fish on his lips.
They put him through a great deal of trouble.

If the fisherman doesn't wet his ass, he won't eat any fish.
We have to work hard to possess the things we want.

The big fish eats the small one.
The strong and capable have authority over the weak.
The survival of the fittest.

The fish stinks from its head.
Deceit and stealing in a group or organization usually starts from the officials.
When people in power or high in office set a bad example for their subordinates.

You're fishing in muddy water.
Your efforts are not sure to lead you to success.

A crab is a great ruler in its hole.
> Even the meek feel like kings in their homes.
> Every man's home is his castle.

He's walking like a crab.
> He is walking slowly.
> He walks sideways.

Catch the lobster and cut its hair.
> It is said about things of little value and of people with minor abilities. We cannot profit from insignificant people or from cheap dealings.

A house guest and fish stink on the third day.
> It is said about people who overstay their welcome.

How much is the crab, and how much is its juice?
> It is said about things that have absolutely no value.

He sent him for green caviar.
> He fooled him.

Without bait, fish can't be caught.
> It is said about businessmen and merchants. If they can't work for the interest of the customer, they have no business.

He caught the eel from the tail.
> It is said about people who take on more than they can actually handle.

He ate my fish and spat on my whiskers.
> This is said when a person shows no respect or gratitude for the help he received.

The fish of the sea don't place themselves in the pan.
> In order to enjoy success and gain profit, we must work hard. Nothing comes easy.

NATURE

If a breeze doesn't blow, no twig will stir.
> We don't act if there's no reason.
> If we don't try, we can never succeed.

Like the sand of the sea.
> It is said in reference to crowded places.
> As the sands on the shore.

No hood is needed for the rain that has already passed.
> When a danger has already passed, precautions are not
> necessary. We have to take precautions before, and not after
> the fact.

A song while harvesting, and a fairy tale in December.
> Everything has it's time and place. In the summer, workers sing
> while laboring in the fields, and in the winter, the cold weather
> is ideal for storytelling to pass the time.

Don't feel proud of the diver when he dives, but when he surfaces.
> We should feel happy and proud at the end of our attempts.

He made a hole in the water.
> He did absolutely nothing. His attempts failed.

The rock that rolls collects no mildew.
> A hard working person is not denied the necessities of living.
> "A rolling stone gathers no moss."

Become the sun, and don't shine on me.
> Be a kind person, even if I don't benefit from it.
> I wish nothing but the best for you.
> This saying reveals true love and respect for someone.

After the thunder comes the rain.
> Before we fail at something, there are always clues of what's
> coming our way, and we should keep a look out in order to take
> certain precautions.
> Learn to read the signs before an approaching disaster.

A steep uphill also has a fast downhill.
> If we try very hard, success is waiting for us.
> Success usually follows difficult trials.

A fine day shows itself from dawn.
> We can usually tell if we will be successful right from the start
> of an undertaking.
> A kind person is noticed from his youth.
> A good character is quickly perceived.

A clear sky doesn't fear lightening.
> A truthful and virtuous person is not afraid of accusations.
> A clear conscience fears no false accusations.

The large ship has a lot of rough sea.
> People in high positions have many problems to deal with.

He has a month that can feed an entire year.
> When a person is able to make a lot of money in a such a short
> period of time.
> When we are able to enjoy a lot of profit so that we don't have
> to worry about working for awhile.

He put the water in the ditch.
> When a person sets his priorities.
> When a person puts his energy and efforts on the right path to
> success.

Water is not carried with a strainer.
> With false efforts and means we cannot profit or succeed.

Where the river walks, from there you drink water.
> We should expect to profit from people who are well off.

**From the small fountain, a person can drink water easier than
from a large one.**
> The chances we are given should be on the level of our abilities.

A person that's wet doesn't fear the rain.
> A person that is used to struggling in his life is able to endure
> many more hardships.

Big rivers spring from small springs.
>Frequently, important people come from humble backgrounds.
>Big achievements and accomplishments start from small things.

Whatever the sky pours, the earth swallows.
>This saying notes the patience and faith that certain people have.

He is flying in the seventh sky.
>He is happy.
>He is in seventh heaven.

He moved sky and earth.
>He did everything to succeed.
>He looked into everything and tried it all in order to succeed.

The ploughman seeks rain, and the potter drought.
>We all want what's right for us.

The one who walks on land and seeks the sea has the devil behind him boiling beans.
>The person who is fine, yet cannot rest and enjoy himself is asking for troubles.

Dry your grass now that the sun is burning.
>Everything must be done at the right time.

From wherever the wind blows.
>It is said about people who are easily persuaded by what other people say and do.
>It is said about people who change their mind and personality depending on the situation.

As the dolphins dance, they invite the sea to become rough.
>This is a type of weather forecast that sailors believe in.

Even if they send you to the ocean, you still won't find water.
>This is about an incapable person who cannot do the simplest task.

Snow of December, August's gold.
>If it snows in winter, the grain harvest will be good in the summer.

When a drop unites with a drop, it becomes a river. A river with a river becomes an ocean.
>   The strength of unity.

Whatever it may rain, may it come down.
>   Whatever will be, it will be.
>   Let things happen, I couldn't care less.

It rained by goat skin.
>   It rained a great deal; It rained bucketfulls.
>   It rained cats and dogs.

He drowns in a spoonful of water.
>   He loses his courage and composure with the slightest degree of difficulty.
>   He is not able to face and deal with the slightest problem.

Don't allow the frog or the little swallow fool you; if the cicada doesn't shrill, it isn't yet summer.
>   You know it is summer when the cicadas begin to shrill.
>   Everything at its proper time.

Even the mountains fall, and the prairies suffer.
>   Even the rich and mighty have their problems and troubles.

The sky and earth united.
>   It is said during a terrible storm when the clouds are so thick and dark that it is hard to distinguish between sky and land.

It rains yonder.
>   This saying depicts indifference.
>   It is said when a person doesn't understand what is going on, or he doesn't give a damn about anything you've said to him.

About winds and water.
>   When we engage in a meaningless conversation.
>   Idle talk, balderdash.

The mountains are used to the snows.
>   It is said about a person who is used to hardships and problems and is able to endure anything in life.

Rainless August, plenty of must (new wine).

The less it rains in August, the better wine the grapes will yield.

After St. Georgios' Day, give your dress air.

Usually, after St. George's Day in the spring, the weather becomes more pleasant.

After St. George's Day there is a period of rest till harvest time.

It's neither hot nor cold.

He doesn't care about it. It doesn't matter to him.

May you be well in August, when the flies are fat.

It is said in jest about dirty and filthy people.

Wind that doesn't bother you, let it blow.

Don't pay attention to the enemies that can not harm you.

If April makes two rains, and March makes one, joy to the farmer who has planted many seeds.

Spring rains make plentiful harvests.

He writes on water and sows in the pond.

It is said about person that does foolish thing of no worth at all.

Also about an undertaking that is marked for failure.

The glory of the sun is different from the glory of the moon.

Day and night have different things to offer.

We do different things during the day than we do at night.

In front there's a cliff, and behind there's a current.

When there is just no way out of a situation.

Between a rock and a hard place.

When we are faced with equally unpleasant alternatives.

The weather has changes.

Things always change. Nothing stays the same.

You're above rivers.

This is said to a person who is acting in an inappropriate manner, or when he says unacceptable things.

One who can drive you mad.

The drowning man grabs his hair.
When we are in severe danger, we want to be helped in any way
possible.

He has midnight now in the afternoon.
It is said about a person who cannot see or understand the most
obvious things.

Night has ears and day has eyes.
What you do during the day is seen, and what you do during the
night is heard.

Their stars did not combine.
They didn't get along.
They reached no agreement.

He praised the mountain and bought the prairie.
It is said about people who praise useless things in hope of
getting something that is useful and profitable to them.

The quiet water pierces the mountain.
With persistence and patience we can conquer many things.

I saw the sun earlier than you did.
I am older than you.
I know more things than you.

Do good and toss it in the ocean.
Do a good deed and don't ask for pay-back.
Do not make a big fuss or noise over a good deed.

If he squeezes the rock, he'll get water.
It is said about the physically strong and capable people.

The deep river doesn't make a stir.
The wise and capable people do not brag about themselves.

Be mindful of a slow running river.
Still waters run deep.

OBJECTS

The cooking pot rolled and found its lid.
> This is said when two people who have a great deal in common find themselves in a relationship.
> It is said when we hit it off with another person.

Glass and luck are easily broken.
> Luck is hard to come by and can easily disappear. We have to take advantage of opportunities before it's too late.

The bad doesn't delay in coming.
> Most of the time, misfortune comes when we least expect it.

Every obstacle for the good.
> Frequently, we encounter an obstacle that can save us from danger that lies ahead.

A wheel that spins doesn't rust.
> Keeping active can only benefit the person.
> When we are active, we are able to gain knowledge through experience and we can perform better.

The poor man's horn is on his forehead, and the rich man's is on his knee.
> The problems of a poor man usually become public knowledge, yet the rich man's problems are likely to stay a secret.

Everything that glitters is not gold.
> Many times, we can be fooled by what we see.
> Something, at first glance, can appear to be of great value.
> Looks can deceive.

When two clay pots are hitting against each other, one will shatter.
> When two people fight or argue, one of the two will come out a loser.

Rome was not built in one day.
> In order for important issues to be settled and major businesses to succeed, hard work and time are needed. When we undertake major projects we must be patient.

If you don't knock on the door, it won't open.
> If we don't ask for what we want, we surely will not get it.
> Seek and you shall find.

The old ship takes on water.
> The elderly frequently lose their abilities with age.
> It is also said about old businesses that are no longer profitable.

Bad news comes running.
> Bad news is quickly known.
> Bad news travels fast.

He came like the Jack of clubs.
> When a person shows up uninvited and creates a disturbance.

With gunpowder, don't go near the fire.
> It is said when we try to keep two enemies away from each other in order to prevent a sure fight.

The pitcher may go for water many times, but it shatters once.
> Sometimes, we attempt to do something very risky, and we succeed, but, if we attempt it again, we may fail.
> Sooner or later, a thief gets caught.

Venice shall not lose a needle.
> It is said when we lose something of no significant value.

The more the cuckold sits, the larger his horns grow.
> The more the husband puts up with his wife's cheating, the more she will cheat.

Let the morelo cherry stay.
> It is said when a person makes stupid and meaningless proposals.

The month that has no Saturday.
> It is said in jest when we refuse to do something.

The pots became censers, and the manure incense.
> It is said when unworthy people are promoted, or praised.
> It is also said about the con-artist who tries to swindle people.

They hung his spoon.
> It is said about a person who arrives late for dinner.

A mill without water won't grind.
> Without the proper knowledge and experience, we can not succeed.

If you don't oil the wheels, the carriage won't run.
> If you don't pay your workers, the job won't get done.

They have him at the canon's mouth.
> They are plotting against him.
> They hate him.
> They are out to get him.

Water and fire can not become in-laws.
> It is said about things that are complete opposites, or about people who are not compatible.

Better late than never.
> It is better to delay doing a good deed than never doing it at all.

Whatever face you show to the mirror, is the face that sees you back.
> The responses we get are based on our actions and efforts.

The wheel turned.
> When things change for better or worse.

The donkey grew and the saddle became smaller.
> The higher our position becomes, the greater our expenses and needs become.

From a small spark a big fire starts.
> Small and insignificant matters can cause great disaster and catastrophe.

Drop by drop, the deep pitcher gets filled.
> With patience and insistence, we can accomplish great things.
> Many littles make a mickle.

He blew off a canon.
>   It is said when a person finds himself in great debt and is not able to pay it off.
>   He went bust, he went bankrupt.

He found it all clubs.
>   It is said when a person finds many obstacles in his way and cannot achieve his goals.
>   He encountered great difficulties.

Some brick oven demolished.
>   It is said when something sudden and unexpected happens.

The one who arrives first at the mill is the one who grinds.
>   The person who takes advantage of an opportunity can profit greatly. The early bird gets the worm.

All roads lead to Rome.
>   All our attempts and actions point to one reason.

I'll make my pestle cry.
>   I don't care about it. It is of no significance to me.

Vicious circle.
>   It's a big mess.

Empty barrels echo louder.
>   The ignorant and foolish people create a big fuss with their stupidities.

Better for my pocket to suffer than my stomach.
>   It is better to not have money than to not have food to eat.

A good mill grinds what it finds.
>   A good and capable person overcomes every obstacle.

You're the last wheel of the carriage.
>   It is said about a person who's presence has no significance.

The knot reached the comb.
> When we can't do anything more.
> When all patience has run out.
> When things have come to a head.

It is a thousand time better to negotiate than to wage war.
> Peace is preferable to war.
> Peace between nations and people promotes social and economic prosperity.

We've become a theater.
> We've made fools of ourselves.

Your paint doesn't pass.
> They don't care about you anymore.
> Your time has passed.

A full stomach has no ears.
> A prosperous person is often insensitive to the problems of others.

Your blood itches you.
> You are cruising for a bruising.

A present cannot be given away as a present.
> You must never give others a present that was given to you.

Too much work consumes the master.
> All work and no play makes life very dull.
> You must take the time and enjoy life.
> Workaholics miss a lot in life.

SEABURN'S POPULAR SAYINGS SERIES

AFRICAN	SEABURN	$9.95
GREEK	GEORGE PILITSIS	9.95
GREEK*	JOHN MENOUNOS	9.95
JAMAICAN (ONE ONE COCO)	J. JOHNSON	9.95
JAMAICAN (BRAWTA)	EDNA BENNET	9.95

100 STEPS NECESSARY FOR SURVIVAL

ON THE EARTH	RM SOCCOLICH	$4.95
IN THE GLOBAL VILLAGE	RM SOCCOLICH	4.95
IN A STRESS ENVIRONMENT	CLIVE WILLIAMS	4.95
JAMAICA	SEABURN	4.95
AMERICA, FOR AFRICAN AMERICANS		4.95

To order any of the above titles, send check or money order payable to Seaburn Books PO Box 2085 L.I.C., NY 11102 or call (718) 274-1300 FAX (718) 274-3353
Shipping: $1.50 for each book
New York and New Jersey Residents add applicable sales tax